"Katie's passion for God's Word is co[...] her heart beats to see women enjoy [...] them to treasure the God of the Word above all else. You will be equipped and encouraged by Katie as she continually points you back to Jesus."

—Gretchen Saffles, founder of Well-Watered Women

"What I love most about this book is that the secrets Katie reveals are not simply steps to rehearse or goals to reach for. Katie digs much deeper to show us how the secrets of a Happy Soul are the unlimited riches *already* deposited in every Christ follower, and she unpacks how to work them out in our everyday lives."

—Jeannie Cunnion, author of *Mom Set Free*

"Katie Orr's *Secrets of the Happy Soul* is a grounded, balanced, encouraging guide for anyone struggling to find happiness daily. I so appreciated her apt handling of the Word of God, coupled with authenticity in her own story. Highly recommended to any woman searching for a joy-anchor in this untethered, pessimistic world."

—Mary DeMuth, author of *Outrageous Grace Every Day*

"If there's one thing I can count on with my friend Katie Orr, it's that the Bible is central to what she teaches. Most important, it's central to the life she lives. I'm thankful to call her my sister, and thankful you're about to join her in her studies. Enjoy!"

—Elyse Fitzpatrick, author and speaker

"Psalm 1 is filled with road language—a pathway for all of us to find the 'right' road. Katie captures this journey in *Secrets of the Happy Soul* by sharing her personal journey toward true happiness found only in God's Word. If your soul is searching for a happy path, this book will help you discover delight along the way."

—Kelly D. King, manager of Magazines/Devotional Publishing and Women's Ministry Training, LifeWay Christian Resources

"Katie Orr is one of my trusted sources for Bible studies, study tools, and biblical wisdom for women. *Secrets of the Happy Soul* is a welcome addition to my bookshelf."

—Christine Hoover, author of *With All Your Heart* and podcast host of *By Faith*

"Katie Orr is a phenomenal Bible teacher. Two things I really love about her: she is relatable and she always points me to Christ. She has helped me in my own daily devotional time in countless ways. You will be blessed by any and all of her resources."

—Jessica Thompson, author and speaker

"A delightfully deep look at what happiness means to God's people. Katie Orr infuses her careful scholarship with practical steps and relatable stories, all wrapped in a warmhearted approach that says, 'We're in this together.' And those six secrets? Worth reading about, worth learning about, and definitely worth telling others about."

—Liz Curtis Higgs, bestselling author of *Bad Girls of the Bible*

"I don't write a lot of recommendations. When I read a book, I want to know that the author has been a good and faithful student, not of life but of God's Word. Katie Orr is that kind of person, that kind of friend, that kind of writer. Katie teaches us more than just what do to, but how and why, reminding us ever so tenderly that life in Christ isn't about doing better but being better—being a Happy Soul."

—Whitney Capps, author of *Sick of Me*

SECRETS
OF THE
HAPPY SOUL

SECRETS

OF

THE

HAPPY

SOUL

Experience the Deep Delight You Were Made For

Katie Orr

BETHANY HOUSE
a division of Baker Publishing Group
Minneapolis, Minnesota

© 2020 by Katie Orr

Published by Bethany House Publishers
11400 Hampshire Avenue South
Bloomington, Minnesota 55438
www.bethanyhouse.com

Bethany House Publishers is a division of
Baker Publishing Group, Grand Rapids, Michigan

Printed in the United States of America

ISBN 978-0-7642-3447-7

Library of Congress Control Number: 2019051181

Cover design by Kara Klontz

Published in association with Jessica Kirkland and the literary agency of Kirkland Media Management, LLC

20 21 22 23 24 25 26   7 6 5 4 3 2 1

In keeping with biblical principles of creation stewardship, Baker Publishing Group advocates the responsible use of our natural resources. As a member of the Green Press Initiative, our company uses recycled paper when possible. The text paper of this book is composed in part of post-consumer waste.

To Chris.
My she-shed builder, kid wrangler,
dinner cooker, and sanity keeper.
I could not have completed
this book without you.
Thank you.
I love you.

Contents

The Happy Introduction   11

Part 1: About the Happy Soul   15

    1. The Pursuit of Happiness   17

    2. Happy! The Name of God's People   35

    3. The Perfect Portrait of Happiness   47

Part 2: The Secrets   59

Secret #1: The Happy Soul Is Focused on God   61

    4. Focused   63

    5. Believe Better   77

    Soul Searching   88

Secret #2: The Happy Soul Is Resolved to Follow God's Way   91

    6. Resolved   93

    7. Grasp God's Way   109

    Soul Searching   120

Secret #3: The Happy Soul Is Attached to God's Word 123

   8. Attached   125

   9. Enjoy God's Word   139

      Soul Searching   149

Secret #4: The Happy Soul Is Dependent on God's Provision 153

  10. Dependent   155

  11. Develop Deep Roots   171

      Soul Searching   183

Secret #5: The Happy Soul Is Confident in Who She Is 187

  12. Confident   189

  13. Pursue Your Purpose   207

      Soul Searching   221

Secret #6: The Happy Soul Is Surrendered to Her King 225

  14. Surrendered   227

  15. Take Refuge   241

      Soul Searching   248

      The Happy Conclusion   251

      Notes   253

The Happy Introduction

From Stagnant to Flourishing

I love to work in my flower garden. I have no idea what to do with cucumbers and tomatoes, but give me a potted plant or a bed of bushes and I'm a happy girl. I love digging things up and moving them around until it all looks just as I think it ought. My favorites lately have been succulents. Thanks to the wonder of YouTube, I've learned how to care for and propagate them (make succulent babies) and keep them thriving.

This wasn't always the case. My first go-around with succulents was an epic failure. I purchased a variety of plants in a super-cool-looking pot, and I set the stunning collection in my living room. For several weeks I enjoyed their beauty. But after a while, the leaves of many of the succulents started falling off at the slightest touch. Some of the stems turned to mush. Other plants were growing really tall, really fast, making them look like a lanky inflatable tube man in front of a car dealership. My once-beautiful succulents quickly became a pot of rotting misfits.

After a bit of research, I gathered that I was overwatering the succulents *and* they were suffering from lack of sunlight. So I moved them all outside to a sunny window box, stopped watering them so much, and waited. The plants started growing again! Even little baby succulents began to show up.

My succulents were *finally* happy.

I'm assuming that you picked up this book because you want to be happy. Perhaps, like my poor succulents, you find yourself in a space that feels less than optimal. The words *thriving* and *flourishing* feel far from your reality. The idea of someone picking you up from your current state of stagnation and moving you to a space where you will thrive sounds simply fabulous.

This book is designed to do just that. Over time, trial and error, and lots of study through the Scriptures, I've discovered the secrets to becoming a Happy Soul, and I'm excited to share them with you.

Now, these secrets may not be what you expect. They are certainly not what I thought they would be. For a long time I figured happiness had to do with a combination of disposition, circumstances, and hard work.

I had heard messages of trying harder to chase down my dreams: Make your ideal a reality.

I had received advice to simply shift my mindset: Make the mental choice to be happy.

I had observed women who exuded a carefree attitude and a continually smiling face. I figured I just needed to be more like these happiness superstars.

But each of these "solutions" I tried (alongside many more) never lasted, if they even worked in the first place. In hindsight, I can see that each attempt tried to fix a sad situation with a temporary and ineffective solution. They weren't getting to the real problem. It was like trying to put makeup on a dirty, ugly pig to make it look like a stunning, graceful swan. A pig is never going to look like a swan, no matter how much you try to dress it up. No amount of cover-up will work to change an identity.

Okay, so I'm not calling anyone here a pig (here's where if we were chatting on our phones, I would add a laughing-with-tears emoji), but I am trying to make the point that these "solutions" for my unhappiness were spiritual makeup at best. They were counterfeits of the real solution.

Secrets of the Happy Soul is not meant to be yet another tube of spiritual makeup used to hide your blemishes. I don't want to provide a way for you to simply strive to become a better, happier person. I want to help you uncover the real and lasting way to happiness.

The secrets I'm going to share with you are indeed actionable and transformational, but they all assume that a massive change— a spiritual rebirth—has already occurred. These secrets are not steps to take to become a Happy Soul. These secrets are the natural movements that come over time from a soul who is Happy—the soul who has been saved from their sin and given great grace from God. A Happy Soul is who they already are. This journey is about working out the incredible, life-changing, happy realities that are true of us because of Christ. So this book is not going to give you a checklist to follow in order to reach a happy status. The truths ahead of us are about understanding the implications of and responses to the soul-level eternal life change provided and proposed to us in Scripture.

Perhaps you've heard the Bible referred to as an instruction manual for life with God. In some ways this is true. However, I think a more appropriate analogy is to see God's Word as the spiritual oxygen we need to stay alive spiritually. Without God and

His Word to us, we suffocate our Happy Soul. When we try to live life without God, we may still have a pulse, but we lack the ability to move forward—spiritually speaking—because we haven't the energy to do much but exist. The deep delight we were created for is right under our nose . . . we simply don't have the sight to recognize it or the strength to pick it up.

This is not the life God designed for us. He came to give us *abundant* life (John 10:10), a *successful* existence (Joshua 1:8), a *Happy* Soul. If this abundant, successful, and happy living is what you crave, I invite you to dive in to the Word of God with me as we search for what He has to say about being a Happy Soul.

I want to show you where your soul should be situated in order to thrive.

PART
1

ABOUT
THE
HAPPY
SOUL

1

The Pursuit
of Happiness

*I have come so that they may have life
and have it in abundance.*

John 10:10

A few years ago an email popped up in my inbox. It was a request from a ladies' group looking for a speaker for their ministry kick-off event. If an event fits my schedule, I typically call the organizer to gather more information about it and to ensure that I can deliver what they want from me. When we got to the topic of my talk, I was a bit taken aback. Typically, I teach through a passage from the Bible that fits the theme of the event and the spiritual needs of the attendees. But this event was different. They wanted me to speak on how I've become the woman I am today.

I had to stifle a laugh.

Not because it was a funny request. People get paid to speak all the time about their amazing success stories—how they made their fortunes, climbed their ladders, slayed their giants. I laughed because I didn't understand why they wanted to hear a happy success story from me. I'm nothing special. I don't have a flashy rags-to-riches story or incredible tale of flight from obscurity to fame. There is no deliverance from addiction or abuse in my story. I have no major rebellions or recklessness I've had to rebound from. I've lived a fairly normal, level life. I have two loving parents who provided for and protected me. I have an amazing godly husband and three healthy, beautiful kids. In other words, my story is pretty simple. My life is not overly remarkable. I am grateful for the life I've lived, but it's not an adventurous one worthy of getting paid to tell the tale.

Right now, I'm very much feeling those same feelings I did a few years ago. This time, it is over you and me and this book. The fact that I'm writing a book about being happy is laughable.

You see, certain people just seem to be born with a cheery disposition. They are satisfied with the small things in life, continually see the bright side, and always smile when they talk.

I'm not one of those people.

Honestly, I tend toward pessimism, dissatisfaction, and discouragement. Depression runs in my family. I'm a pastor's wife who wakes up some days and doesn't want to go to church. I've been on medication for depression. Twice. There are days I loathe my body. And there are plenty of days I don't want to get out of bed. I yell at my kids, and then I hate myself for it. I lost my twenty-nine-year-old brother to a drug overdose, and the waves of grief from that loss still slam me to the ground. I've cried myself to sleep. My default is to see every glass as half-empty. I also notice the smudges on cups and the teeny specks in the water.

These (and more) are reasons why I shouldn't be able to write this book.

This is me in all my glory: Unhappy Katie.

However, there is good news—and it's glorious. Unhappy Katie is Old Katie. And Old Katie is dead. The Bible tells me that as a Christian, "I have been crucified with Christ, and I no longer live, but Christ lives in me" (Galatians 2:20). So, yep. Old Katie is dead and now there is a New Katie! "Therefore, if anyone is in Christ, he is a new creation" (2 Corinthians 5:17).

New Katie is content.

New Katie loves people.

New Katie isn't shaken when her world falls apart.

New Katie is patient and kind.

New Katie has an insatiable desire for God and His Word.

New Katie is a Happy Soul.

This talk of my "old self" and "new self" might be confusing. It was to me at first. But the more I spent time reading my Bible, the more I saw what it taught about my spiritual rebirth. And the more I understand what the Bible teaches about being born again, the more I see these realities play out in my own life. One of these new-birth realities is this: God has made me a Happy Soul.

I've been a Happy Soul now for almost three decades, and I've learned a thing or two on my Happy journey. After searching the Scriptures, I see what God has to offer the soul that *feels* less than happy. I've experienced a soul-level satisfaction and joy as I've chosen to take God at His Word and follow in His Way. Not perfectly. Not consistently. But over time I have experienced the fullness of being a Happy Soul.

Though I will share my story with you, I want to provide you with more than just what has worked for me. I want to give you timeless, proven biblical principles and promises. I want to point you to the Author of those principles and the Guarantor of those promises. Because if all I give you is my story and my thoughts and my opinions, then all I can offer you is a laughable example to follow. But if I can somehow lead you closer to the God who has declared me a Happy Soul and led me to live that declaration out, then perhaps these words can be more than just ink and paper. Perhaps they can be the beginning of your own breakthrough.

A Deeply Delighted Creation

Do you have any recurring dreams? I've had one particular nightmare for as long as I can remember. The environment sometimes differs, but the core of the dream is that I'm unprepared and panicked. Typically, I scurry to study for an exam, yet each time I sit down to study, some upheaval occurs. My book disappears, my notes are unreadable, or (the worst-case scenario) I realize I've been enrolled in a class I didn't know about and I'm super behind. But when I try to go and catch up on the course, I never can find the classroom.

Panicked, I run myself ragged. I repeatedly attempt to study and make it to the test in time, but I am unsuccessful, again and again and again. Then (here's the kicker), somewhere along the way, I realize I've been studying and searching all over town in my birthday suit! It is here when this dream of mine delivers the double-whammy of shame. I am stripped of my dignity. I fail at my pursuit of perfection. I wallow in a puddle of pity . . . until my iPhone alarm mercifully jingles me awake.

Ages ago, mankind experienced a real-life nightmare that shattered perfection and introduced incompleteness. Genesis 1 and 2 tell us that God created the world and saw that it was good; man and woman, land and sea, plants and animals were all present, complete, and perfect. They were perfectly holy and utterly happy.

He planted a paradise, with the perfect temperature, the sweetest fruit, and the very presence of God to delight in.

Did you catch that? The Creator of *everything* walked the earth and enjoyed His creation. And all of creation enjoyed Him. God was satisfied with the earth and everything in it, and they were satisfied in Him. Sin was nonexistent; shame was not an issue. Adam and Eve walked around naked! It is impossible for me to imagine any scenario in which being unclothed and unashamed could be true. Even within a safe and healthy marriage, I prefer to be covered up. There is a visceral vulnerability that comes with nakedness, even when there is no good reason to feel that way.

Yet here we have Adam and Eve, who felt nothing wrong with their situation. In their state of flawlessness they had no need for concealment—and this perfection was not solely a physical one. There was nothing but excellence and fullness, satisfaction and celebration, harmony and bliss for these two human beings. They had no unfulfilled longings or unmet needs. Disorder, deterioration, and discord were not in their vocabulary. Adam and Eve were wholly happy . . . for a while.

You've probably heard what happened. Through the first act of sin—a decision which at its root doubted the plan and character of their Creator—Adam and Eve fell from flawlessness. Their independence and disobedience immediately swept them away from the bliss that was all they had known: endless delight, personal perfection, and a comprehensive satisfaction in God and His good plan. Through this fall from flawlessness came far-reaching physical, emotional, and spiritual ramifications that extended to the rest of mankind. That includes you and me. And so our spiritual DNA has been forever altered, and now death, disease, and discontentment are our default.

Though we've lost the perfection of paradise, the longing for this Golden Age remains. God created mankind to be absolutely happy. Our cravings were completely satisfied in Him and our feelings perfectly directed by Him. Pleasure was abundant. Peace and contentment ruled. Though the benefits of Eden were lost, a desire for perfection, a longing for satisfaction, and a craving for contentment and pleasure lingers. These are all leftover cravings for a perfect garden relationship with our magnificent God, and they are existent within every soul. Yet because we are stained with sin, we can no longer enjoy the unhindered presence of God, and our yearnings are trapped within us. These dissatisfied longings point us to all that was shattered through the fall. And now, we are each, in our own unique ways, attempting to fill the void that was once filled with the presence of God who walked in the perfect garden with His people. Yet we also each have the consuming stain of Adam within us, a propensity to forget the goodness of our Creator and His excellent plan, and so we try to satisfy these innate longings through things other than the companionship and comfort of our Maker. We have a tendency to ignore our lack of ability to get things right, and downplay our need for a much better way than what we are currently experiencing.

We are all seeking out the original state of perfect human Happiness.

The Need for Transformation

If you were to pull up into our home's driveway, to your right are huge split-leaf philodendrons. These resilient plants cover a lot of ground, and their large leaves make dramatic, long-lasting fillers for my vases indoors. However, much to our frustration, they keep growing out and into our driveway. Behind them is a good six to seven feet of potential ground for them to take over, yet they keep leaning in toward the driveway. With their four-foot stalks, they impede our ability to drive up and down our driveway without running into the plants. We've pruned them time and time again, but they just keep coming back.

When you take a step back and look at our house from across the street, you can see that old oak trees cover much of our yard, especially on the side of the driveway where the philodendrons are. From that perspective, we can easily see why they keep moving into our driveway: The plants are slowly yet continually inching out of the shade. They reach and reach and reach, trying to grab all the goodness of the sun they can get. Why? Because they are happiest in the sun. If you have certain houseplants, you can see this in action as well. Oftentimes, the plants will twist and turn to lay out their leaves in the space where they can catch the most sunshine—because the sunshine makes them happy.

Just like these eager residents of Kingdom Plantae, you and I are constantly searching for what will help us flourish—so much so that we will turn and bend to expose ourselves to find what will make us happy. The problem is, we don't always recognize exactly what will bring us true and lasting growth. Our sense of direction is often off and we chase after the promise of pleasures that never truly satisfy.

If you and I could get honest—really honest—with one another, I think we would both admit that deep down we hold an innate dissatisfaction with life as we know it. Yet so often our Facebook feeds tell a different story. I get it, who wants to update their status with "I really hate my life right now"? Sunday mornings at church are not much different. There have been so many times where the last place I wanted to be was in a room full of smiling faces asking me, "How are you?" Because I know that most of them don't *really* care to know how I am in that moment. Or if they did, in the middle of the right aisle, two pews from the back, doesn't feel like the best place for me to break down in tears. It just becomes easier to pretend everything is simply great, while a deep dissatisfaction looms.

This longing manifests itself in so many ways. But if we take a long, hard look at what it is we really want, we'll see that what we really want is to be back in the perfect garden with our Creator. Because it is only in His presence that we are completely delighted, perfectly peaceful, and absolutely satisfied. My soul longs for happiness. Your soul longs for happiness. Every soul on this earth longs for happiness. But on our own, we will never find it. Nothing and no one will bring lasting, soul-level satisfaction. So we keep leaning and longing until we find the paradise we are looking for. There is a massive something that keeps us from experiencing the fullness and delight of Eden; this barrier keeps us from the deep delight we were created for.

My alma mater is Auburn University. Known for its Southern charm, deep traditions, and over-the-top hospitality, Auburn, Alabama, has been dubbed the Loveliest Village on the Plains, and it holds a very special place in my heart. The traditions of Auburn are sacred to the Auburn family. Undoubtedly, the most unique tradition of Auburn University is that of "rolling" Toomer's Corner. This is where, after an athletic victory, thousands of crazy fans descend to the intersection of Magnolia and College—where the corner of campus meets downtown Auburn—and we throw rolls of toilet paper into the large oak trees until it looks like a winter wonderland. As those old oak trees are rolled, fans chant cheers, sing the alma mater song, and celebrate until they're too tired to stand. As crazy as it sounds, it is a staple in an Auburn fan's life. We win, we roll!

Sadly, in November of 2010, the eighty-five-year-old Toomer's Corner trees were dealt a mortal blow when a disgruntled University of Alabama (Auburn's biggest rival) fan quietly poisoned the Toomer's Corner oak trees. Using a strong herbicide, the Alabama fan sealed the fate of those lovely live oak trees. The man, known as "Al from Dadeville," called in to a radio show to brag about what he had done, saying, "They're not dead yet, but they definitely will die."[1]

No one knew the trees were in trouble until the crazy radio rantings were confirmed by soil testing. Every effort was made to save the trees, and though the trees looked fine, they were indeed doomed. The trees had been killed the instant the poison entered the soil. The beloved Toomer's Corner trees were eventually removed, the soil wholly replaced, and new trees planted in their place. No amount of physical work could save those trees. This was devastating news to the Auburn community.

Unfortunately, you and I are in a similar situation. Because of the fall of Adam, we each find ourselves in polluted soil. And as long as we exist in this sin-stained soil, we are spiritually dead. I know this isn't good news. Nor is it fun coffee shop conversation. But it is biblical. It is our reality. I doubt that sin has ever been a fun topic to address, but it is certainly super hard to talk about today. The moment any mention of "right" and "wrong" is detected, red flags are raised by the world around us, and the condemning labels of "exclusive" and "closed-minded" are slapped on our backs. Yet the Bible is clear that there are rights and there are wrongs. Sin *is* a reality, not a social construct. Therefore, we all need an intervention. Without rescue, any pursuits toward "flourishing" are worthless. We may seek to clean ourselves up, and make ourselves better. But no amount of bending toward the light or cleaning up our leaves will work. As long as we are planted in polluted soil, any efforts made toward becoming a Happy Soul are worthless. This all sounds stark and hopeless, but through the rescue of Christ, *good news abounds*! There is a way out of our polluted soil.

Through Christ, we are transplanted. Through Christ, we receive rebirth.

What It Takes to Become a Happy Soul

During His earthly ministry, Jesus often taught hard-to-understand spiritual realities through parables—stories of spiritual truths through physical examples. In the book of John, chapter 10, Jesus uses the analogy of a door to explain how He provides a flourishing life for those who would seek it. "So Jesus again said to them, 'Truly, truly, I say to you, I am the door of the sheep. . . . If anyone enters by me, he will be saved and will go in and out and find pasture. The thief comes only to steal and kill and destroy. I came that they may have life and have it abundantly'" (John 10:7, 9–10 ESV). Here we learn that Jesus came to bring us (we're the sheep in this object lesson) three things: salvation, pasture, and life abundant. These first two, salvation and pasture, lead to the latter: life abundant.

Through Jesus Christ, the sheep receive salvation: protection from what seeks to destroy them. The sheep also enjoy the provision of the pasture, where they will find ample food and water, continual safety, and rest. It is through both the shelter and the bounty of Jesus that the sheep obtain the life He came to give them. The word *abundantly* here means a life "beyond the norm."[2] This is not referring to the physical life that everyone has. It is an exceptional, extraordinary life. This "beyond the norm" abundant life, green pasture, and eternal salvation Jesus promises is obtained through Him: the door of the sheep. And here we arrive to the first reality about becoming a Happy Soul: It starts with the work of God.

Becoming a Happy Soul takes a work of God

Throughout the Old and New Testament there is an important thread of teaching about a covenant relationship between God and His people. Covenants were an important part of life in that day and age, and God used their familiarity of the formality of covenant agreements to communicate His commitment to them. From Genesis to Revelation, we are taught that God is a faithful, merciful, righteous God who desires to be in a relationship with mankind and also to bless His people with His presence. Throughout the Bible we see that God offers us an abundant, beyond the norm, full life through entering into a covenant—an eternally binding—relationship with Him. The Happy Soul life starts with entering the "door of the sheep." It is through this door—a recognition of our need for Christ—where we find the place in which we were created to flourish. Jesus is the gateway to paradise. "My sheep hear my voice, and I know them, and they follow me. I give them eternal life, and they will never perish. No one will snatch them out of my hand" (John 10:27–28).

The Bible also makes it clear that Jesus is the way, the truth, and the life (John 14:6). He is not *a* way, *a* truth, *a* life. He is *the* only way to know God. He is *the* only ultimate truth. He is *the* only way to abundant life. Therefore, our Happy Soul journey must start with Jesus. He is the door to the Happy life we seek.

This life is beautifully portrayed in Psalm 23. You've probably heard this promise-filled poem before. Read it again today, slowly, looking specifically for all we gain through a covenant relationship with our Good Shepherd.

> The Lord is my shepherd;
> I have what I need.
> He lets me lie down in green pastures;

he leads me beside quiet waters.
He renews my life;
he leads me along the right paths
for his name's sake.
Even when I go through the darkest valley,
I fear no danger,
for you are with me;
your rod and your staff—they comfort me.
You prepare a table before me
in the presence of my enemies;
you anoint my head with oil;
my cup overflows.
Only goodness and faithful love will pursue me
all the days of my life,
and I will dwell in the house of the Lord
as long as I live.

Psalm 23:1–6

No wants.

Still waters.

Restoration.

Nothing to fear.

Comfort.

Food on the table.

Overflowing provision.

Unshakable goodness and immovable mercy.

The very presence of God.

Now, don't you think that sounds like the makings of a Happy Soul? Doesn't this look like the good life we're searching for? Once again, we see a description of life beyond the norm for the sheep who enter into the protection of the Shepherd. These promises are primarily spiritual, not physical. Spiritually speaking, when we enter through the door of Christ, we find protection, provision, and the extraordinary life. We are not to read these verses and assume that we are promised protection from cancer, car accidents, or other calamity. Nor are we promised a healthy bank account, a full belly, or all our dreams fulfilled. However, *eternally* speaking, we can be free from fear, perfectly provided for, and enjoy life everlasting.

Here's the bottom line: We can never be happy without God in our life. And by "in our life," I'm not talking about simply changing the music we listen to, attending church, and adding a few Christian titles to our bookshelf. I'm talking about a life change. A rebirth. A soul-revolution. Through Christ, the status of our soul moves from dead to alive, condemned to forgiven, orphaned to adopted, chosen, beloved, and blessed. Through Christ alone we can become a Happy Soul.

As you read these words, you may be nodding your head, saying, "Yes!" and "Amen!" You have experienced this new birth and there is no doubt in your mind that you too have been declared righteous by our Holy Judge. You know where you will be for eternity, and you look forward to that day when you will see your Savior face-to-face. If this is you, rejoice! Though the excitement and joy and fulfillment you may see in other Christians seems to elude you, regardless of how you *feel* in this moment, if you are in a relationship with Jesus, you are already on the Happy path. The Happy Soul life is not reserved for the super-spiritual. There are no classes of Christianity. All of God's promises are for all of God's people.

Now, perhaps you're scratching your head, not quite sure if all of this is actually what you've experienced. Maybe you walked forward at a church service long ago and repeated a prayer someone dictated to you, but you're not quite sure if it "took." Perhaps you've grown up in church most of your life and have always considered yourself a Christian, but you don't feel very close to God. Or maybe you've just recently begun attending religious services or exploring Christianity through books, and you're hoping that your actions might demonstrate to God that you're interested in Him. These are all great actions to take! However, these actions do not and will never save you. The Bible clearly teaches that we are not saved by our works—we do not earn eternal salvation through good actions. This is actually a comforting truth—because I get it wrong all the time! One day I may have a "good works" day, but the very next day I choose poorly. Salvation is not based on what we do. Salvation is based on what Jesus Christ has done for us. This is indeed extraordinarily good news.

Salvation is a gift of grace from God. Grace is unearned and freely given. In this case, the gift of grace is the sacrifice of Jesus on the cross, which paid the penalty our sin deserved. Every sin deserves a punishment and separates us from a holy God. Jesus' gift of grace has the ability to restore the garden-relationship with God. We can now hold on to the promise of one day experiencing His presence as Adam and Eve once did.

The Bible calls this gift of grace the Gospel—the good news about what Jesus has done for us. Since Jesus has already lived a perfect life and has already paid the penalty of our sins, we don't need to wait until we have the entire Bible read and figured out to receive this gift. We don't have to clean ourselves up before we come to God. Through the Gospel, we can receive both forgiveness and cleansing from our sins, and therefore a renewed eternal relationship with God.

It's important that we get this straight, because knowing we have eternal security affects our every moment. If we live uncertain of our destiny, it will rob us of our joy, our peace, and a sense of purpose. If you want to be a Happy Soul, it starts with the eternal security we receive through entering a relationship with Jesus. It begins when we know Christ personally—not just know *about* who Jesus is, but really know Him. This eternal security doesn't rest on anything we have done. It all depends on what Christ has done for us—His great work of grace. Our only part is faith.

> For everyone has sinned; we all fall short of God's glorious standard. Yet God, in his grace, freely makes us right in his sight. He did this through Christ Jesus when he freed us from the penalty for our sins.
>
> Romans 3:23–24 NLT

Being a Happy Soul takes a work of faith

I was born a Christian . . . or so I thought. I grew up in Christian school and have always been around God's Word and God's people. I have early memories of summer Vacation Bible School puppet shows and my Precious Moments Bible. I attended Wednesday night kids' programs at church and got all A's in Bible class. I caught on to the do's and don'ts of Christianity and followed them faithfully. I knew "the prayer" of salvation—I'd heard it a bazillion times and prayed it several times myself. I thought I comprehended what it took to become a Christian. But I was not a Christian. I went to Christian school, I did Christian activities, and I said Christian things. But what I didn't get was that doing all the Christian things and knowing all the right answers wasn't enough. Knowledge didn't make me a Christian. Going to a Christian school didn't make me a Christian. Being a good girl didn't make me a Christian. Deep down, I knew I was missing something . . . but didn't quite know what it was.

I knew *about* Jesus but I didn't *know* Jesus. I knew *about* His death on the cross, but I wasn't trusting in Christ to take care of my sin problem. I had been trusting in the knowledge and good-ness of Katie. I had been trying to take care of my sin problem through being good and doing right. Gratefully, one day I realized that it is not enough simply to know intellectually that Jesus came to save me from my sins and give me the "life beyond the norm" He promised. I had to do something about it. I had to respond. And one afternoon, sitting in my bedroom, that reality hit me: I didn't really know God personally. So then and there, sitting on my forest-green-and-maroon paisley bedspread, I recognized my need for rescue and that Jesus was the only one who could save me. Through this first act of repentance and surrender, I went from death to life, from sinner to saint, from hopeless to Happy.

Looking back, I can see that before my salvation moment, I didn't really think I needed saving from anything. I was a pretty good girl who often thought, *Are my sins really bad enough that Jesus needed to die for them?* I knew all about Jesus and the cross, but I didn't depend on it because I didn't really believe I needed it.

My first action of faith started with a recognition of my sin problem. We all have a sin problem. We all need rescue. And all we need in order to be rescued is to place our faith in our only hope: Jesus.

> For you are saved by grace through faith, and this is not from your-selves; it is God's gift—not from works, so that no one can boast.
>
> Ephesians 2:8–9

Being a Happy Soul takes a "working out"

Sears, Roebuck and Company used to sell a product called the Modern Home. Between 1908 and 1940, over seventy thousand of these fully sized houses were purchased and delivered.[3] Yep, you heard me correctly: Customers could browse the catalog, pick out their perfect floor plan, and a build-your-own-home kit would be delivered to the customer via train. Once the home arrived, the new homeowner had all the materials needed to create their dream home. Their house had arrived, but there was still much effort put forth to make their dream home a reality.

Through faith in the work of Christ, our Happy Soul "dream-home kit" has arrived, but there is still work to be done in order to bring it to full realization. It took me a very long time to realize this. I thought that because I had salvation, I would no longer struggle. I believed that the Christian life was supposed to be easy and that my soul should be *automagically* filled with happiness and joy, fulfillment and success. However, I missed all the Bible verses that state that this life on earth is hard, experiencing and enjoying God takes cultivating, and this world is not my permanent home. One day, when I am in the unhindered presence of God, I will be content and fulfilled 100 percent of the time. But now, as I wait to see Him face-to-face, I get to join God in the work He is doing in and around me to build me up into the Happy Soul He's created me to be.

This is what Paul meant in his letter to the church at Philippi when he told them to "work out your own salvation" (Philippians 2:12). Just like some members of the builder generation put together their mail-order Modern Homes, we have work to do to build the Happy Soul life God has gifted us. All the materials we need have been paid for in full, and we are officially "happy homeowners." With the grace of God as our foundation, the work of Christ as the doorway, and the Word of God as our blueprint, we can move forward in the construction of our Happy life.

> For we are his workmanship, created in Christ Jesus for good works, which God prepared ahead of time for us to do.
>
> Ephesians 2:10

2

Happy! The Name
of God's People

How happy is the one . . .

Psalm 1:1

Depending on your background, you may be scratching your head a bit by now, wondering how all this lines up with sermons you've heard or books and blog posts you've read. Perhaps you grew up hearing that God doesn't care about our happiness, but that He definitely cares about our holiness.[1] There is a dichotomy frequently presented between pleasure and piety. I've heard this again and again within Christian circles. For example, a popular marriage book boasts the tagline, "What if God designed marriage to make us holy more than to make us happy?"[2] This thought that God wants us to be holy more than He wants us to be happy is pervasive.

However, there are many modern leaders who take the position that happiness is a worthy pursuit. Most notably, John Piper presents a theology that holds happiness as something every Christian ought to pursue; a deep, abiding joy is found in seeking God as our greatest treasure.[3] Many of our Christian forefathers, including C. S. Lewis and Jonathan Edwards, were in favor of the pursuit of happiness, and taught that God gives happiness freely.

Another point up for debate is whether *joy* and *happiness* are synonyms or separate entities. Many teach that joy and happiness are indeed two very different words, and hold that Christians ought not to seek happiness, but instead pursue joy. They state that Christians must "be careful when we come to the text of the New Testament that we do not read it through the lens of the popular understanding of happiness and thus lose the biblical concept of joy."[4] They teach that happiness is of the world, it is simply a fleeting emotion that ought not to be pursued, whereas joy is biblical.[5]

However, other teachers just as influential make the case that there is little to no distinction between joy and happiness, they are of the same essence and the "terms are synonymous in their effect and too difficult to distinguish. . . . To rob joy of its elated twin, happiness, is to deprive our soul of God's feast."[6] Some argue for a parallel relationship with the words happiness and joy, and assert that joy and happiness are "virtually interchangeable" and believe that it is "needless, distracting, and misleading to make fine distinctions between joy, happiness, gladness, merriment, and delight. They all speak of a heart experiencing the goodness of God and his countless gifts."[7]

Confusing, right? If the really, really smart people who know what they are talking about and have studied the Bible intensely can't come to agreement, what hope do we have of figuring it out? I respect each of these teachers and their thoughts. I think they are all within biblical teaching. Yet there is a very strong polarization present when it comes to the teaching of happiness. Thus, we're receiving mixed signals.

I put out a (super-duper official) poll on Facebook asking women if they have heard any of the following:

A. God doesn't care about your happiness; He cares about your holiness.

B. Happiness is not something we should pursue. Joy is.

The overwhelming majority (91 percent) had heard of at least A or B. I asked ladies to simply leave an A and/or B in the comments if they'd heard either, or to comment C if they'd heard neither. Interestingly, 32 percent also commented with reasons why they agreed with the teaching they'd received against pursuing happiness, even though I didn't ask for it. There are some strongly held opinions on this topic.

I think much of the confusion stems from semantics—what one person means when they use the word *happiness* is not the same as what the other means in their usage. Additionally, the further back we go through the teachings of our spiritual grandparents, we encounter a similar problem. What they meant by using a specific word choice then is not what that word means now. We're all using the same word—happiness—but what the speaker (whether modern day or from past generations) intended by the word is often different from what the listener receives from it. This is what linguists call semantic drift—words that were used in everyday conversations centuries ago but mean something very different today.

Happiness is not the only word subjected to this semantic drift. For example, the word *awful* originally meant "worthy of respect or fear."[8] In Old English, *meat* held a much more general meaning of "food, nourishment, sustenance," and didn't come to mean the specific type of food—the flesh of animals—until the 1300s.[9] *Bimbo* used to mean fellow.[10] A *husband* was a homeowner.[11] *Sad* meant satisfied.[12] *Intercourse* simply suggested "social communication between persons" until the late 1700s.[13]

Interesting, right? As amusing as these changes are, these linguistic evolutions lead to confusion. So we need to figure out: Is happiness a subjective experience or an objective state of being? Is it a fleeting feeling or a foundational truth? Is happiness a gift from God to be received, or is it even promised in the Bible at all? Or could it be some combination of the above? Once we know the answers to these questions, we can know how or even if we should pursue happiness. In order to better define the meaning of true happiness, let's see how the Bible sheds light on the reality of Christian happiness. There are already comprehensive books out there that go deep into the biblical teaching of happiness, so I'm not going to recreate the wheel. Instead, I want to focus on one important spoke of that wheel, and it is found in the Psalms.

Happy: The Name of God's People

I hold a science degree from Auburn University. I loved studying all things biology, anatomy, parasitology, and all the other -ologies. One thing you learn quickly: Every living organism has a very specific name. You've heard about this before. It's where we get *Homo sapiens* from. Of all the creatures I've studied, *Cryptosporidium hominis*, *Staphylococcus aureus*, and *Naegleria fowleri* were some of the bacterial and parasitic pathogens (the bad guys) that were fun to pronounce. The fancy terminology for this naming system is known as binomial nomenclature. This taxonomy system is based on Latin names that correspond with the Genus and species of each organism. My favorite plants all have these fancy names too: *Agapanthus africanus*, *Magnolia soulangeana*, and *Gardenia gummifera*. These classifications tell us exactly "who" these plants and organisms are. We may call them by their nicknames, but their binomial name is who they really are.

Happy is what we are called

The Old Testament holds an oft-missed truth about the name of God's people. This truth is uncovered in a Hebrew word found most famously in Psalm 1:1: "Blessed is the man . . ." Most translations (as seen here in the English Standard Version) start Psalm 1 with the word *blessed*. A handful of Bible translations utilize *happy* instead (Christian Standard Bible, Good News Translation, New Revised Standard, to name a few). If we dig deeper and look at the original manuscripts in Hebrew, we discover the word אַשְׁרֵי (pronounced "ash-ray"). This word literally means "oh, the happiness," and clues us in to the purpose of these collected poems. One of the very interesting things about this "happy" word אַשְׁרֵי is that it is an exclamation used to proclaim the status of that person. It's like that person just walked into the room, and the author blurted out, "אַשְׁרֵי!"

"Happy!"

This Hebrew word is used forty-five times in the Old Testament, and almost thirty of those are found in the Psalms. Our happy word אַשְׁרֵי ("ash-ray") refers to both an internal state of being and an external emotive reality. It is used to describe one who enjoys "a heightened state of happiness and joy, implying very favorable circumstance and enjoyment."[14] So it's internal and external. It has a show-and-tell quality about it. It is a status that is evident as well as integral. To be אַשְׁרֵי ("ash-ray") is both part of her skin and part of her soul. God's people are אַשְׁרֵי! God's people are Happy!

To make sure you and I are understanding the same meaning, from here on out, I'm going to capitalize Happy whenever we're talking about this biblical אַשְׁרֵי ("ash-ray") Happiness.

Happy is who we are

My favorite tree is a saucer magnolia tree—the type I climbed as a child in my grandparents' backyard. I can identify other saucer magnolia trees through their overall shape and size, as well as the shape, size, and color of the leaves and the pink blooms it puts out in spring and summer. I know a saucer magnolia tree (*Magnolia soulangeana*) by the way it looks, but if I had a bag of magnolia seed in front of me, I wouldn't be able to tell the difference from the saucer magnolia (*Magnolia soulangeana*) and the southern magnolia (*Magnolia grandiflora*). Trees, just like humans, have DNA and can be identified through DNA testing. So if I couldn't distinguish the seeds from one another and I *really* needed to know if it was indeed a *Magnolia soulangeana*, DNA evidence could tell me.

Happiness is not something we pursue, it's something we are. It's in our spiritual DNA.

I am a woman.

I am green-eyed.

I am 5'8".

I am a brunette. (With lots of gray!)

I am a B+ blood type.

I am a Happy Soul.

The Happy Soul, ideally, is both an internal and external reality. It is who we are and what we look like. It is part of our spiritual DNA as a child of God, and it is an external evidence that shows who we are. The Happy Soul has both internal and external ways of being identified. If you are in Christ—if you have taken that first step of faith to cling to the work of Christ on your behalf—then you are אַשְׁרֵי ("ash-ray"). Always and forever, this is your name.

אַשְׁרֵי = The internal name of God's people

אַשְׁרֵי = Our spiritual Genus and species

אַשְׁרֵי = The Happy Soul

And if we look at all the arguments about happiness vs. holiness, and joy being greater than happiness, seeing Happiness as a name instead of an emotion puts it all to rest. It agrees with those who say we shouldn't chase down trying to be happy; we see that we are *already* a Happy Soul, so there is no need to waste our time pursuing a fleeting emotion. Our external status may not always match up with that internal reality, but "Happy!" we are. Always.

Understanding the Stages of Our Happy Soul

When was the last time you saw a newborn baby? There is typically such hope and excitement surrounding a new life. An infant is the epitome of potential. Especially for parents and grandparents, there is an invigorating anticipation in watching that perfect little bundle of joy grow and develop into all they can be. Great care is taken to feed the body and soul. Why? Essentially, it is to help the expression of their genetic code. We don't typically put it this way, but when we nurture a human being from birth, our hope is that they will reach their full potential physically and intellectually.

When it comes to our spiritual life, Christians hold within them the same amazing potential. We are also all in need of the same nurturing. Our internal identity doesn't instantly match up with our external reality. Regardless of how you feel right now, deep down within your spiritual DNA, you are Happy. Through the greatness and grace of God, there is potential within you for the amazing, abundant, "beyond the norm" Happy Soul existence.

However, depending on how much this internal reality has been nurtured, what you experience externally might be far from Happy. It's almost like the opposite of many Facebook statuses and Instagram feeds. Social media portraits are never a true representation of real life. Conversely, as Happy Souls, our reality is beautiful, but the picture others see is off from our internal, incredible Happy Soul reality.

Basically, we are all a work in progress. It is uber-important that we understand the process that is our salvation. Because once we understand the game plan and the role we have to play in executing it, we can dive in with both feet and join God in the work He is doing within us. The Bible teaches that there are three stages to God's rescue of our souls.

God has rescued me.

God is rescuing me.

God will rescue me.

Through Christ we are given an immediate present (justification), a continual pursuit (sanctification), and an eternal promise (glorification). We live in a state of "already, but not yet" when it comes to our salvation.[15] We are already saved, but not yet.

I have been saved.

I am being saved.

I will be saved.

Let me show you what all this means.

God has saved me from the penalty of sin

In the moment that I trusted Jesus to pay the penalty of my sin, that magnificent moment that I became a Happy Soul while sitting on my paisley bedspread, I was justified. And now, when God looks at me, it is *just as if* I had never sinned. Through Christ, the penalty of my sin has been paid, and the righteous, obedient life He lived out on this earth has been imputed (big word for "credited into my account") to me. Jesus took away my sin; it was nailed to the cross and paid for through His death. Then, through the same power demonstrated when He resurrected from the dead, He gifted me His perfect life. So when God looks at me, not only does He *not* see my sin (which is huge!), He *sees the perfection of Jesus* (which is even more huge!). Justification is an immediate and irreversible gift of forgiveness and right-standing before God. The Christian—the Happy Soul—is forever and fully justified through Christ.

> Therefore, since we have been declared righteous by faith, we have peace with God through our Lord Jesus Christ.
>
> Romans 5:1

> The righteousness of God is through faith in Jesus Christ, to all who believe . . . They are justified freely by his grace through the redemption that is in Christ Jesus.
>
> Romans 3:22, 24

God is saving me from the power of sin

From that moment on, as brand-new justified Happy Souls, we enter into the next stage of our salvation: sanctification. Justification was instant. Sanctification is gradual. Justification took away the punishment of sin. Sanctification takes away the chains sin has wrapped around us. This is the process of becoming more and more like Jesus. This is where our internal reality of righteousness becomes more and more of an external reality. Unfortunately, many Christians never engage in this part of their transformation. But it is through the process of sanctification that we see our two realities—internal and external—begin to grow closer and closer to one another.

There is a deep connection between our daily experience of Happiness and our daily pursuit of holiness. They are, in fact, two sides of the same coin. The Happy Soul is a Holy Soul. The Holy Soul is a Happy Soul. She has been declared righteous and she spends her life's work showing off the righteousness of Christ to the world around her. As the "sanctifying work of the Spirit" (1 Peter 1:2) breaks us free from the patterns of sin we've been walking in, and as we cooperate with God's work in our lives and "walk in newness of life" (Romans 6:4), over time we begin to look more and more like the Happy Soul He's created us to be.

> How happy are those whose way is blameless,
> who walk according to the LORD's instruction!
> Happy are those who keep his decrees
> and seek him with all their heart.
>
> Psalm 119:1–2

> As obedient children, do not be conformed to the desires of your former ignorance. But as the one who called you is holy, you also are to be holy in all your conduct.
>
> 1 Peter 1:14–15

> [You] were taught by him, as the truth is in Jesus, to take off your former way of life, the old self that is corrupted by deceitful desires, to be renewed in the spirit of your minds, and to put on the new self, the one created according to God's likeness in righteousness and purity of the truth.
>
> Ephesians 4:21–24

God will save me from the presence of sin

Through justification, we have been freed from the penalty of sin. Through sanctification, we are being freed from the power of sin. But there is more. One day we will be absolutely free from the presence of sin. The Bible calls this our glorification. When we take our last breath and leave this earth, we will stand face-to-face with Jesus in heaven, and an incredible transformation will occur. The Happy Soul knows and clings to the fact that ultimately, this earth is not our home. Instead, "our citizenship is in heaven, and we eagerly wait for a Savior from there, the Lord Jesus Christ. He will transform the body of our humble condition into the likeness of his glorious body" (Philippians 3:20–21).

Like our justification, this is a part of our salvation that fully rests on the power of God. Our role is to cling to the hope we have in these promises. One day, we will be perfectly Happy. There will be no worries or woes—only fullness and joy. There will be no wants or unfulfilled wishes—we will be completely content and absolutely satisfied. We will enjoy the unhindered presence of God, just as Adam and Eve did ages ago in the garden. We will once again experience the deepest delight and the highest happiness. With sin obliterated and shame vanquished, all disorder, deterioration, and discord erased, we will walk in perfect union with our incomprehensibly glorious and holy Maker. And our souls will be wholly, gloriously, ridiculously Happy.

> On that day it will be said,
> "Look, this is our God;
> we have waited for him, and he has saved us.
> This is the LORD; we have waited for him.
> Let us rejoice and be glad in his salvation."
>
> Isaiah 25:9

> They will no longer hunger;
> they will no longer thirst;
> the sun will no longer strike them,
> nor will any scorching heat.
> For the Lamb who is at the center of the throne

will shepherd them;
he will guide them to springs of the waters of life,
and God will wipe away every tear from their eyes.

Revelation 7:16–17

I know we've explored some big words and deep concepts. But it is critical that we understand what has gone on, what is going on currently, and what will occur because of the salvation we have in Christ. The gospel changes everything about us, but if we continue on as if nothing has changed, then we forfeit the immediate blessings Jesus died to bring us. We don't have to wait to see Him in heaven to enjoy the benefits of our salvation. We have been given a new identity, a new name. And with this change comes incredible transformation.

Justification.

Sanctification.

Glorification.

All of this from Him who called us to salvation.

All of this for the one called Happy.

Happy are the people with such blessings.
Happy are the people whose God is the Lord.

Psalm 144:15

3

The Perfect Portrait
of Happiness

He is like a tree planted beside flowing streams
that bears its fruit in its season and whose leaf does not wither.
Whatever he does prospers.

Psalm 1:3

The Bible has lots to say about our well-being, satisfaction, peace, joy, flourishing, and more. I wish we could walk together through the entire counsel of Scripture and learn all there is to know about the Happy Soul living. However, we simply can't cover it all in 256 pages. But what we can do is zoom in to a passage that teaches about the good life God has planned for us. We can study several verses that will give us the essence of what the Happy Soul life looks like. And for that, we will turn to the Psalms.

Have you ever read a psalm and felt as if it was written just for you? This Old Testament book contains the records of both praise and lament from God's people long ago. Though they lived in a different place and time from you and me, they were people who experienced the same joy and sorrows as we do. Filled with declarations, questions, confession, requests, and more, the Psalter has been intricately woven within the history of God's people. For many, it is their go-to place to read when they are not sure where to go. It is an inviting book.

The book of Psalms is a collection of 150 Hebrew poems that inform us not only of who God is, but also how to worship Him and walk in His ways through the redirecting of our hearts, minds, and souls. The Psalter points out to us what is already clear in the rest of Scripture, but here we uniquely encounter theology (what we believe about God) with artistic emphasis and raw emotion. Feelings are declared honestly and liberally by the poets; requests are made boldly, often with great desperation.

As their ancient journey unfolded, the Israelites responded to their God through the singing of songs.[1] "When the psalmist experienced God's love and salvation in his life, he sang with hymns of joy. When he experienced hardship, he composed a lament. When God answered his petition, he thanked God. When he saw God enter history once again to be with His people, he recounted the long history of God's relationship with Israel."[2] As these prayers of praise and songs of lament were spoken and sung, an oral tradition was carried on from generation to generation. Many of the psalms assume a congregational presence, most likely in a formal worship setting, while others point to a more personal plea. These were eventually written down, gradually collected, and finally organized into a book we now know as the Psalms.[3] From the time of Moses (Psalm 90) to the return of God's people from exile (Psalms 126 and 137), this Old Testament book includes psalms penned from a span of at least nine hundred years!

You and I get to hold all this history of struggle and rejoicing in our hands. As we follow in the footsteps of our forefathers of faith, the book of Psalms is a beautiful, practical guide for us as we learn how to respond to the character and actions (or seeming inactions) of God. The book of Psalms is simultaneously a telling of theology and a bleeding book of raw emotion. It is a safe place for our messy hearts to land, to receive healing, and to be refocused on the steadfast love of our God. Yet the Psalms are more than just a bunch of words to help show us that we are not alone."The book of Psalms is an instruction manual for living a truly happy life."[4] The Psalms give us instructions on how to become the Happy Soul—not only in name but also in practice.

The Essence of the Psalms

Though they've been around for centuries, essential oils have taken the 2010s by storm. Aromatherapy used to be found primarily in the homes and wellness plans of the super-crunchy, but oil-filled diffusers have now found themselves on many counters of the average American—including mine.

My favorite essential oil is lemongrass. My husband thinks it smells like Froot Loops! It has a sweet, refreshing smell; I love diffusing it to mask cooking odors and bring a fresh fragrance to the house. Another favorite aroma of mine, especially before bed, is lavender. A lavender plant sprawls outside our front porch gate, and when it is in full bloom, you can catch a whiff of its fragrance. Yet just a tiny drop of lavender essential oil gives off an exponentially stronger scent than the large bush does.

In a bush of lavender, there are roots, stalks, leaves, and other fibrous material. A vial of oil contains only the extract of the plant. Everything else has been stripped away. Only the essence of the lavender remains—the unique and wonderful scent of the plant that makes it what it is.

Together, Psalms 1 and 2 are considered the introduction to the rest of the Psalter. They are the essence of the Psalms. This gateway introduces us to the major themes to be found again and again in the words throughout the 150 Psalms. The Psalm 1 and 2 duo is like a trailer for the blockbuster movie. We're going to dive in to both psalms in the pages ahead, but before we do, I want to point out one structural element.

> How happy is the one . . .
>
> Psalm 1:1

> . . . all who take refuge in him are happy.
>
> Psalm 2:12

Our Happy word אַשְׁרֵי ("ash-ray") is at the beginning of Psalm 1 and then again at the end of Psalm 2. The Psalms are filled with this purposeful poetic signaling. I like to think of this particular one as a Happy Soul sandwich. It begins and ends with the promise of Happiness, and these two small chapters begin to reveal to us the meat one can enjoy in the rest of the Psalms.

The Secrets Revealed

I hate spoilers. If I think you are about to tell me something about a storyline I've not yet enjoyed to completion, I'll plug my ears and proceed immediately with singing, "la-la-la-la-la-la-la." Even though I hate spoilers, I'm going to let you in on the Happy Soul secrets right now, because I want you to know where we are heading.

Secret #1: The Happy Soul is focused on God.

Secret #2: The Happy Soul is resolved to follow God's Way.

Secret #3: The Happy Soul is attached to God's Word.

Secret #4: The Happy Soul is dependent on God's provision.

Secret #5: The Happy Soul is confident in who she is.

Secret #6: The Happy Soul is surrendered to her King.

On the back of this book you can view my headshot photo. This is the picture that is supposed to be the best current representation of me. It is not a picture of me just waking up in my jammies, with bedhead and no makeup on. I'm guessing that if you have any sort of social media platform, you didn't select the first selfie you came across for your profile picture. You selected a flattering photo to represent who you are. Beyond our profile pictures, many see social media as an opportunity to show off the best parts of ourselves. When we think of something clever, see something beautiful, or are so proud of something we can't stand it, we share it! It is not often that you see pictures of a messy house, screaming and/or fighting children, a dirty toilet, or our dying plants. We typically stick to the snapshots that celebrate the beauty in our lives.

This introduction to the Psalms is the snapshot of Happiness. It's the ideal. It's the family portrait where everyone is smiling and perfectly placed. It is the best-dressed, most beautiful version of God's people. It is a picture of what we could be here on earth as well as a promise of what we will be in heaven.

If אַשְׁרֵי! ("ash-ray") is our name, the Happy tree here in Psalm 1 is our portrait. It is a visual example of what the Happy Soul is like: a well-rooted, abundantly fruitful, incredibly resilient tree. This is the portrait of the ideal. The best version of ourselves. Strong. Beautiful. Vibrant. Happy. But we must be careful not to turn these secrets into a checklist of creating our own happiness.

The Unhappy Pendulum of Trying Harder

After I became a Christian, I didn't have anyone there telling me what to do next. I knew something was different within me, but all I knew was to keep going with all the do's and don'ts of which I'd made a collection. Though spiritually I was different, practically speaking, I carried on the same way: as if it all depended on me.

Before I became a Christian, I was trying to earn God's favor.

After I became a Christian, I sought to prove myself good enough for God's favor.

Before I became a Christian, I followed all the rules so that God would accept me.

After I became a Christian, I followed all the rules so that God would keep me around.

What I didn't understand was that the grace of God is not merely for the moment of salvation. The grace of God is for a lifetime of walking with God. Unfortunately, there is much teaching floating out there that perpetuates these lies. On the surface they sound good, but ultimately they encourage things that are counter to Scripture. I see at least two main dangerous teachings prevalent in today's Christian circles: rigid religion and powerful personhood.

Rigid religion tells us to follow the man-made righteous rules and don't ask questions. You don't need to know why, just do it. Go to church. Stop smoking. Change your company and your wardrobe. Read your Bible. Serve others. If you aren't changing, it's because you are not giving God your all.

Try harder. Do better. It's all up to you.

On the other end of the pendulum is powerful personhood. The rules are new, but the demands are the same. Decide who you want to be, and be her. Stay true to yourself. If you aren't changing, it's because you are not giving it all you've got. Get it into high gear.

You are enough. Shift your perspective. Do what feels right. Recite your positive-thinking mantras. You got this. You do you. Go on, get out there—be the hero of your own story.

The crazy thing is, both sides of the spectrum hold some biblical truth. Many of the actions dictated are found in Scripture: take care of your body, make efforts toward growing into a better person, shed the actions and attitudes that keep you from growing, live a disciplined life. Any life well-lived will include intentional choices and hard work. However, there is a fundamental flaw if our goals are pursued without the power of God as our fuel and the glory of God as our motivation.

Both of these ways of try-harder living are rooted in the elevation of self. This is not what the Bible teaches. What these messages lack is the power of God. If you hear a sermon or read a "christian" book that gives you all of the to-do's but nothing about the power of God as a necessary undercurrent or the ultimate goal of displaying God's glory, perhaps it's not really Christian after all.

Living the Happy Soul life will never be by our efforts alone.

For far too long, I measured spiritual growth by my external actions. I thought that the person with the longest list of do's and don'ts checked off wins the Greatest Christian trophy. Trying hard shows you're a good Christian. Giving up the list is a Christian failure. That used to be me, the legalistic rule-follower. (And the tendency remains to this day.)

After years of attempting to keep up with all the actions I thought I needed to do in order to become a really good Christian, I began to veer in my choices. The do's and don'ts had become more and more wearisome. I was tired of being the good girl. I wanted to experience life to the fullest without the hindrance of regulations. Poor choices pounced on my weary will to be good. Some of those choices became public knowledge, and the news of my actions spread like wildfire throughout school. Word got around that I was not the good girl everyone thought.

The news reached a brave friend of mine. He approached me with the rumors. I listened to his gentle rebuke: "Are these things true? People look up to you, Katie. They are watching you. You are supposed to be an example of what it looks like to walk with Christ." The answer I gave him rings loud in my head to this day: "I really don't care anymore."

Those words escaped my mouth, and a part of me (the part that was tired of the good-girl, try-harder life) was incredibly relieved to get it out in the open. I was done. Tired. Completely exhausted by the do's and don'ts. Yet there was a whisper of something in me—deep down inside my worn-out heart—a small cry saying, "No! That's not true! I do care. This is sin, and it hurts me and it hurts others and it hurts the heart of God. I don't want to go down this path. I truly want to obey God." I stood stymied after that encounter with the friend who loved me enough to confront me with my sinful choices. I didn't know exactly where to go next, but I was beginning to see that something had to change.

For years, I thought that in order to obey God I had to follow all the rules and keep myself clean. But in that moment—burdened by the try-harder life—a new desperation for God's presence rose up within me. I began to see that my hunt for righteousness through works was futile. It only took a few weak moments of rebellious choices to tear down the image of Katie I had poured years into building. I didn't yet know exactly what change looked like, but I could hear God's Spirit speaking gently to me: "There is another way. You need me. Trust in me. I'll show you the way."

A revolution had begun. I was at the end of myself. I was at the beginning of surrender. I was ready to leave the try-harder, do-better, control-more life behind me.

The Problem with Trying Harder

This try-harder cycle starts with a need to change behavior, a longing for "victory over sin." So we start our list:

Do this.

Don't do that.

Take a look around to see who seems to have their ducks in a row.

Add what she does to the list.

If all of that doesn't work, look for a "better" church with a "better" pastor.

Try a conference. A retreat. A new book. Another Bible study.

Find an accountability partner.

. . . try, try, and try some more.

People and tools certainly have a part to play in our personal growth (and I am in no way suggesting that we stop going to church, reading our Bibles, etc.). However, the best preacher, the greatest tools, and our most sincere efforts cannot change our hearts. Effort spent on the cycle of trying harder leads to frustration, and failure, and it will never produce true and lasting change. It is impossible to keep this "wheel" going. It might take days, weeks, or years, but failure always comes, leaving us fully deflated and feeling guilty.

There are two primary destinations of this trying-harder approach. Many can manage to keep this wheel going most of their Christian life, but they end up exhausted, prideful (and often cranky and judgmental) souls who don't experience the grace of God in their day-to-day living. More common are the people who eventually see the futility of their pursuit of perfection; they recognize that they will never be able to change. So they give up the cycle altogether. They quit trying to change themselves, stop coming to church, give up reading their Bible and the pursuit of being a "good" Christian. They do not experience the grace of God in their day-to-day living.

Trying harder either leads to tidy self-righteousness, pride, and no need for God, or it leads to exhaustion, disillusionment, giving up, and outright rebellion. Both of these results of the try-harder wheel are rebuked in Scripture, yet we who've grown up in church often focus more on avoiding the latter and run straight to the deeds of the former. Self-righteousness looks a lot better on paper than rebellion. But the inward struggle of pride and self-dependency is just as repulsive to God. Jesus abhorred self-righteousness. It was the behavior he rebuked again and again, during His time on earth. So we must be careful not to turn "Christian living" into a self-help slogan in order to seek a spiritual status that doesn't actually move us closer to God.

You may wonder why it matters what our motives are. As long as I'm doing good deeds, doesn't that please God? Actually, no. It's not solely about our actions. Our motives absolutely matter. Trying harder with the wrong motives leads us to build our own shrine, where people can look and say, "Wow, look at her!" Our actions ought to point others to see God's greatness, not our own. Self-righteousness is the antithesis of God's glory, and I was stuck in self-righteousness for a long time. My view of God was teeny tiny, and my view of self was grossly inflated. No wonder I didn't experience the fullness of life that comes with intimacy with God! I was too absorbed in making myself "better" and showing others my "good" works to enjoy the presence of God.

Here's the hard reality we need to come to grips with: Trying harder lacks the ability to bring spiritual transformation. Don't hear me wrong—the Christian life takes effort. It's hard work. But you and I can practice the exact same "spiritual disciplines" (reading our Bible, going to church, prayer, etc.) and reach much different results, depending on the fuel behind our efforts. The key to realizing "success" in the Christian life is not in trying harder. Intimacy with God is found as we believe better. As our view of God grows, our actions naturally follow suit. Our desires change. The same list-checking pursuits become a way to worship our precious Savior for whom we've grown to become profoundly grateful. He is beautiful to us. He is powerful, in control, and intimately acquainted with our moments. When we focus our efforts on responding to the character of God, becoming partners of His powerful work within us, and understanding the good and grand calling on our life, a true and lasting revolution of our moments occurs.

Reaching Our Full Potential

My husband and I once spent a summer in East Asia on a mission trip. We had an amazing time and enjoyed immersing ourselves in the food and culture. Asians, generally speaking, have "short" genes—shorter in stature than, say, Europeans. However, there were several elderly women we saw who were remarkably short. Because the country we were in has a history of oppression and suffering for their common people, especially for those of the older generation, I wondered if malnutrition played a role in their exceptionally short stature. Of course, there is no way of knowing without speaking to them. While genetics certainly has a part to play, if they did not have the nutrition needed to thrive as a child, they may not have lived up to their full potential in height. This phenomenon is found to be true throughout many periods of history. The average height of people who lived before the modern age of abundance and medical advancements is much shorter than the average height of people today. For many countries, like America, the problem of malnutrition of the masses is behind us. Most of us are now living up to our full physical potential.

This is the essence of what this book is all about. I want to help you see how our actions—directed, fueled, and empowered by God—result in a full-grown and mature Christian. This way takes work, but it is work that is guided, fueled, and course-corrected by God. Walking down this way is hard and different from this world's definition of right, but this is the way to our full potential in Christ.

Are you ready to dive deeper into this full-potential portrait? We're going to take a closer look at the Happy Soul portrayed in the Psalms. This will not be a step-by-step guide to being happy; these secrets are not sequential stepping-stones to a better life. These are characteristics of the Happy Soul displayed in Scripture. They are very much intertwined with one another as a holistic pursuit, and woven into the fabric of the heart that knows, loves, and serves God.

From here we get to dive into each secret, one by one. For each we'll look first at the biblical teaching, then we'll turn our hearts toward practicalities. In the next section of the book, we'll be answering these questions:

What does the Bible have to say about how to be a Happy Soul?

What does this look like in my everyday life?

What is keeping these Happy Soul secrets from becoming Happy Soul realities for me?

I'm truly thrilled you're taking this journey with me. Let's dive in. It's time for Secret #1.

PART
2

THE

SECRETS

SECRET #1

THE HAPPY SOUL
IS FOCUSED
ON GOD

4

Focused

You are good, and you do what is good;
teach me your statutes.

Psalm 119:68

I vividly remember the first time I was seriously unhappy. My heart was heavy with the realization that some of my relationships were not as they seemed. The sting of betrayal and neglect left my heart broken and bruised. A heaviness depressed me for days.

One afternoon during this dark season of the soul, I felt an urge to read my Bible. It wasn't much of a habit of mine at the time, but I dusted off my copy and opened up to a random passage. After flipping around for a bit, I landed in the Psalms and began reading. My heart leapt at these words:

> My tears have been my food day and night . . .
> Why are you in despair, O my soul?
> And why have you become disturbed within me?

Hope in God, for I shall again praise Him for the help of
    His presence.
O my God, my soul is in despair within me . . .
The LORD will command His lovingkindness in the
    daytime;
And His song will be with me in the night . . .
Why are you in despair, O my soul?
And why have you become disturbed within me?
Hope in God, for I shall yet praise Him,
The help of my countenance and my God.

Psalm 42:3, 5–6, 8, 11 NASB

Yeah, so my "suffering" was nowhere near the severity of the psalmist, but the brutal reality of his desperation and the honesty in which he declared it penetrated me. Those words on the page in that moment put names to the state of my soul—feelings I'd assumed I was alone in: disturbed. Shattered. Despondent. And the fact that these emotions were right there, on the pages of Scripture, made me feel as if maybe my emotions weren't simply bad feelings I needed to hide . . . and maybe God has something to say about my feelings. I didn't have all the answers, but I felt comforted after reading this Psalm.

Sadly, that comfort didn't last. Though the honest truths in Psalm 42 touched me in that moment, they didn't truly penetrate my soul. My heart remained easily shaken by the actions of others—and it would be for a long time, because my hope was still being placed in people and how they viewed me. (I can still fall quickly and easily into this trap.) And though I found immense solace in knowing that my emotional struggles were not unique to me, I missed the bigger picture of this psalm. I was primarily reading with self-centered eyes. I was placing myself in the psalm, looking for the to-do list, and missing what my soul truly needed—the anchoring, consoling, eternal truths in Psalm 42 of *who my God is.*

Isn't it easy to fixate only on what we want changed instead of fixing our eyes on the only One who can bring change? If I had looked for what I could learn about God, I would have seen that He is a living, personal God. His presence brings me hope and help. My heart would have been comforted with the knowledge that God is powerful and kind, steady and loving. Because when we fail to look for God on the pages of Scripture, we miss the main point. We miss seeing the very Person whose nearness brings the comfort and joy we seek.

Life Is Lived Better with God at the Center

> This is what the LORD says:
> The wise person should not boast in his wisdom;
> the strong should not boast in his strength;
> the wealthy should not boast in his wealth.
> But the one who boasts should boast in this:
> that he understands and knows me—
> that I am the LORD, showing faithful love,
> justice, and righteousness on the earth,
> for I delight in these things.
>
> Jeremiah 9:23–24

I told you we would study Psalm 1 and 2 in order to see the secrets of the Happy Soul, but there is one secret we need to uncover first before we head there. This secret is embedded in the very fabric of what the Bible is: a special revelation of who God is. But so many of us miss this important point. The Bible is not a collection of stories about mankind. It is not a history book. It is not a how-to guide for how to live our lives. It is first and foremost a book about God. It is theological in function and form. Does it include history? Indeed. Does it record stories of people from whom we can learn? Yes. Does it give us instructions for how to live our lives? Absolutely. But all of it—every story, every rule, every historical detail—is there to point us to God.

If there is any sort of quick fix when it comes to becoming a Happy Soul, it is this: We need to get our focus off ourselves and turn it to God. And the primary way we know about God is through the Bible. That means starting from the correct vantage point. Instead of turning first to what the Bible can *give* us and what we ought to *do*, let's start with a resolve to *see God more clearly* in the pages of Scripture. For so long I read the Bible primarily through the lens of "What does this mean to me?" The Bible does mean so much to me, as I'm sure it does to you too. However, this is not the best first question to ask when we approach God's Word. The more appropriate question—and the one whose answers I've found to bring the greatest comfort and lasting joy—is, "What does this teach me about who God is?" This is the primary purpose of the Bible: to specifically reveal to us the character of God.

Worried about how you are going to pay your next bill?

Set your gaze on God, your Provider.

Afraid of what's around the corner?

Remember God, your in-control King.

Have you been wronged by someone?

Look to God, our righteous Judge.

In the throes of one of your darkest seasons of the soul?

Focus on God, our comfort through the storms.

For so many of us, this is counterintuitive. When something isn't right in our lives, we want to know what to *do* in order to fix it—and we want to do it *now*. For so many years, the thought of "looking to God" felt like a non-action to me. Perhaps you feel the same way—that the action of opening your Bible in order to learn more about who God is is not actually helpful when your world is falling apart. Because "put your focus on God" can seem like a weak and useless platitude when you're drowning. But it is especially during the hard times when we need to know—really know—the steadfast character of our God.

This is not to say that we simply "look to God" and everything magically falls into place. But *really* seeing God for who He *really* is will always be the starting point for the Happy Soul. If your soul is stuck in despair or fear, hopelessness or pain, the right and best next step is always to remember the faithful, unchanging, good character of God.

The Happy Soul is focused on who God is.

How to Focus on God

The primary way we can focus on God is through the Bible. We call it the Word of God for a very good reason: That is exactly what it is. The Bible is a *specific* and *special* revelation from God. Now, there are things He has *generally* revealed to us through nature. When we stand at the end of the ocean, we can get a glimpse at God's enormity and power. When we enjoy the beauty of a flower in all its intricate design, we can see the artistic hand of our Creator. When we observe the complexity of the human body or the specificity of the tilt and rotation of each piece of the universe, we can behold the amazing attention to detail by their great Designer. But without the Bible, there is no specific evidence for knowing exactly who this Creator is. We need the Bible—God's Word—to give us the fullest picture of that Creator.

Let's go back to that first time the Bible brought me comfort. Seeing that I was not alone in my struggle through the words in

Psalm 42 was like receiving a warm blanket for my cold and weary soul. I am thankful for the comfort I received that day through the story of the psalmist, but my situation didn't change overnight, and it didn't take long before I had allowed that blanket of truth to slip off my shoulders. It wasn't a conscious decision to let it go, but it wasn't a deliberate choice to keep clinging. So the emptiness once again permeated my heart. Perhaps you've had a situation of your own, where initially a Bible verse brought you comfort, but it didn't seem to go with you through the rest of the storm.

Before I understood the power of knowing and trusting in God, I treated the Bible like it was my security blanket. I pulled it out when I needed an extra comfort or pick-me-up. I was content to use it as a Band-Aid for my boo-boos, when I could have enjoyed the very healing and companionship of Christ. There—in the presence of God—I would have found true rest and comfort, with the powerful arms of God wrapped around me. Though He has been and always will be with me through every stage and season of life, my moment-by-moment experience of His abundant power and faithful presence will be determined by the way I treat His Word.

The Bible is so much more than a collection of moral examples and rules to follow. It is an invitation to daily see God more clearly and to dwell in His presence. God's Word is not to be primarily used like I had utilized it for so long—as a pop-up shelter in the midst of a storm, to be forgotten and left behind once the clouds have cleared. No! Understanding God's character through Scripture is the gateway to the very presence of God. Clinging to the character of God invites us to dwell in a secure, heated house in the midst of the blizzard.

The Bible is not our security blanket.

The Bible is our secure connection to our Creator.

As you and I stop using the Bible as a way to get a quick pick-me-up and start enjoying God's Word in order to know God better, we will experience the stability that comes with establishing that deep connection.

As we move past treating the Bible as a spiritual help desk, we also need to make sure we are not placing ourselves at the center of God's plan. The Bible is not primarily a book about Adam and Eve, Ruth and Naomi, or Martha and Mary. Nor is it all about you and me. The Bible is a book primarily about God, and if we fail to recognize this, it causes a reading (and therefore incorrect understanding) of Scripture that is mankind-centered instead of God-centered. We take a quick peek at the characters of the Bible and attempt to place ourselves in their shoes. We seek out the commands and turn them into a be-a-better-Christian checklist. Yet we so often miss the bigger picture because we neglect to intentionally look for God on the pages of Scripture.

The Happy Soul is focused on who God is.

Focusing on God Brings Unclaimed Benefits of the Bible

A few years ago, my husband, Chris, was looking through his benefits package for some needed info. As he was searching the website, he noticed something about a vision plan. After additional rooting around, he found that we have a vision plan that covers annual exams. Sadly, we had been paying out of pocket for our annual exams for at least ten years! The benefits were ready and waiting for us to claim, but we didn't even know they existed.

This is what we do when we fail to look for God in the pages of Scripture. We miss out on the benefits of who He is. Now, don't hear me wrong. I am not saying that He is a vending machine God, who dispenses out what we want if we do the right things. The end goal of studying the Bible is not to give us a tidy, happy life. The end goal of studying the Bible is to know God better and enjoy Him more and more. Studying Scripture is the best way to learn more about who He is. So much of what we seek—a joy-filled heart, an unexplainable peace of mind, and a satisfied soul—is found as a by-product of being with Him because, whether or not we realize it, deep down our souls cry out with the Psalmist, "My soul thirsts for God, for the living God." And that thirst will only be satisfied as we get to know God better through the pages of Scripture and experience the benefits of His character.

Turning our attention to the grandeur of God—and away from self—is a difficult task that requires a lifetime of intentionality. Though it is difficult, it is also simple: Take my focus off myself and put it on God. Here are just a few of the benefits promised to us when we shift our focus to God.

Keeping our gaze on God brings abundant peace, joy, hope, and more

> You will keep the mind that is dependent on you
> in perfect peace,
> for it is trusting in you.

Isaiah 26:3

Now may the God of hope fill you with all joy and peace as you believe so that you may overflow with hope by the power of the Holy Spirit.

Romans 15:13

For whatever was written in the past was written for our instruction, so that we may have hope through endurance and through the encouragement from the Scriptures.

Romans 15:4

A firm hold on God's presence through His Word brings great comfort

> Even when I go through the darkest valley,
> I fear no danger,
> for you are with me;
> your rod and your staff—they comfort me.
>
> Psalm 23:4

> This is my comfort in my affliction:
> Your promise has given me life.
>
> Psalm 119:50

> Blessed are those who mourn,
> for they will be comforted.
>
> Matthew 5:4

Blessed be the God and Father of our Lord Jesus Christ, the Father of mercies and the God of all comfort. He comforts us in all our affliction, so that we may be able to comfort those who are in any kind of affliction, through the comfort we ourselves receive from God.

2 Corinthians 1:3–4

Knowing God and following His good plan brings blessing

But seek first the kingdom of God and his righteousness, and all these things will be provided for you.

Matthew 6:33

> Trust in the Lord and do what is good;
> dwell in the land and live securely.
> Take delight in the Lord,
> and he will give you your heart's desires.
>
> Psalms 37:3–4

This is just the tip of the iceberg. There is a direct relationship to our view of God and our experience of all He's promised us.

The Happy Soul is focused on who God is.

Seeking a Bigger View of God

I'm a pastor's wife. Which means I'm around a lot of church people. The sad reality about some of us "church people" is we often do not look like Christ at all. I could write another book on all the sad and crazy stories I have experienced and heard while ministering to the church. There have been many times that I have wondered if some church members actually do know Jesus. They say and do some really ugly and hurtful things and don't seem to think their actions and words are a problem. God's people are not perfect, but we are to be growing. Yet it seems that some hearts are more wrapped up in controlling how they look and getting what they want than they are with knowing God better.

The reality that breaks my heart is that many churchgoers are not actually Happy Souls. There are people who are surrounded by the things of God—His Word, His church, etc.—but they actually do not know God personally. I can't see inside the heart. Only God can. But if we are looking for evidence that someone is a Happy Soul, and we start with some outward evidence that the focus of their hearts is on God, the proof of salvation is nowhere to be found.

Or perhaps some are like I was—a Happy Soul in hiding for a full decade before the telltale signs of growth began to show. You see, I thought that being a Christian was all about being good, showing up, doing the right things, and not doing the wrong things. But I was missing something huge: My view of God was not growing. I was more focused on cleaning myself up and proving myself good than I was focused on knowing God and what He had planned for my life.

Being a Happy Soul is not about going through the "good Christian" motions. Being a Happy Soul is about knowing and worshiping God. And the Happy Soul who is consistently putting her focus on God will be a soul who looks like Christ everywhere she goes. She's been in the Word of God and it shows. As she places a high view on the Word of God by opening it, enjoying it, obeying it, and sharing about it, people see the evidence of God in her life.

The Happy Soul is focused on who God is.

The Gold Standard for Measuring Spiritual Growth

> But grow in the grace and knowledge of our Lord and Savior Jesus Christ. To him be the glory both now and to the day of eternity.
>
> 2 Peter 3:18

I'm a C. S. Lewis fan, as you might also be. I've enjoyed the CHRONICLES OF NARNIA several times . . . and I think it might be time to do so again soon. This series tells the tales of several children as they explore the land of Narnia and encounter new creatures and wild adventures. Throughout the series is Aslan the Lion, the King above all High Kings. In *Prince Caspian*, Lucy, who encounters Aslan after several years of not seeing him, declares:

> "Aslan," said Lucy, "you're bigger."
> "That is because you are older, little one," answered he.
> "Not because you are?"
> "I am not. But every year you grow, you will find me bigger."[1]

If we polled one hundred Christians and asked them how they could tell if someone is growing in their relationship with God, we might get a hundred different answers. There probably would be some general categories we could group them all into, and most of them will be external actions and attitudes. They stop cussing. They go to church. They love difficult people. But the problem with solely relying on the external to determine if someone is growing is that actions can be faked and attitudes can be feigned. Motivations are not always evident. I lived a decade of good-girl Christianity, but my view of God hadn't changed much at all. My view of God was off. My view of God wasn't growing.

Have you ever been sick, or had symptoms and Googled them to see what is wrong with you? Every time I have tried to diagnose my problems through the internet, I end up with a list of a dozen diseases that I could have. So many diseases have the same symptoms. Once I head to see my doctor, she typically orders labs that will provide her with additional *internal* information in hopes of shedding light on what might be causing my symptoms. In some cases, there are "gold standard" tests that provide the best way to prove the presence of a pathogen or determine the patient's level of a hormone, electrolyte, or blood cells. If the gold standard diagnostic test is positive, the doctor can walk forward in confidence of the treatment plan.

Just as the doctor cannot typically diagnose the patient's reality by observing only external symptoms, so we cannot measure our spiritual reality solely from external show, because the gold standard of spiritual health is not what we look like on the outside. The ultimate measure of spiritual maturity is found in our view of God. Not church attendance or the cessation of cussing. Not our giving records or memorized Scripture. This is not to say that our external actions don't matter. They absolutely do! But true spiritual growth always starts with the seed of beholding the magnificence of God. And as our view of God becomes more and more accurate, so will the reality of our daily lives reflect more and more of Him. These external changes *will be true* of the Happy Soul, but they stem from an internal knowing of and trusting in God's character.

Focusing on God is not a one-time action; it is a lifelong pursuit. And as we seek to know God better, He will become bigger and grander and more dear to us than ever before. Therefore, the Happy Soul is a consistent learner of God, and her view of God is growing into a more accurate portrait of who God is. Like Lucy with Aslan, every year we find God bigger. He is more powerful and magnificent than we can imagine; He is more faithful and merciful than we can hope for; He is more righteous and holy than we can grasp.

5

Believe Better

*Know that the LORD your God is God, the faithful God who keeps
his gracious covenant loyalty for a thousand generations with
those who love him and keep his commands.*

Deuteronomy 7:9

A few weeks ago I took the kids to Disney's Animal Kingdom
amusement park. One of our favorite rides there is Kilimanjaro
Safaris, which is a guided open-air truck tour of the African sa-
vanna. Unlike most Disney rides, there are no animatronics or
special effects here. The ride is a twenty-minute drive through live
animal habitats. There are lions and hyenas, hippos and rhinos,
elephants and cheetahs. My favorite are the giraffes. Since we have
Florida resident annual passes, we get to see them often, and there
are several adorable baby giraffes we've been watching grow up.
Each tour you take is slightly different, as the animals have freedom
to roam. Plus, the safari tour guide is different every time, and
they each have their own unique tales to tell. One guide we had

recently shared that giraffes can start walking within thirty minutes of birth—that's over 10,000 times faster than humans are able to walk! Newborn giraffes almost literally hit the ground running.

We've chatted at length about the importance of knowing better who God is through the Bible. But here's the problem: Most believers haven't been taught how to study their Bible in a way that is fruitful in their pursuits to know God better. On top of that, we often expect to be able to hit the ground running when it comes to understanding the Bible. Yet when we open and read our Bibles, it is confusing instead of clear. We feel like we should be running but instead we are tripping all over ourselves.

I wish you and I could sit down for a couple hours and get to know one another. I'd love to hear your story. Specifically, I'd love to hear what your experience in the Word has been like of late. Since we can't, I'm going to start at the beginning. If you are further along than just starting out, awesome. Feel free to skim quickly until you find your place in this progression. But whether you are brand-new to the Bible or a seasoned studier, we are all somewhere on the road to better Bible study and the journey of knowing God better.

Bible study is a skill; we must learn to strengthen our spiritual muscles and coordination in order to start taking steps toward biblical literacy. We are not baby giraffes. We are not born—spiritually speaking—with the innate and complete understanding of how to walk with God through the study of His Word. And it is difficult to move forward in our efforts to believe better if the Bible continually confuses us. So we need to take some time to figure out how to strengthen those leg muscles so we can take the next step. Because better Bible study will help us believe better things about God.

I've worked with thousands of women to help them on their journey toward better Bible study, and there are three main roadblocks I commonly see. First is the lack of a regular habit of being in the Bible. Next is having trouble understanding what we're reading once we're there. And last is the tendency to keep our "Bible time" separate from the rest of our lives. We forget what we've encountered in the Bible and fail to allow it to affect our everyday. Let's take a closer look at each of the barriers and how we can overcome them.

Build the Habit

> Imprint these words of mine on your hearts and minds.
>
> Deuteronomy 11:18

> This book of instruction must not depart from your mouth; you are to meditate on it day and night.
>
> Joshua 1:8

Raise your hand if you've started reading through the Bible but lost steam somewhere in Exodus. Yep. Me too. Perhaps you have a bunch of half-completed Bible studies sitting on your shelves like I do. Or maybe you've been too intimidated to start at all. If any (or all) of these describe your experience, you are not alone in this struggle. This hurdle of inconsistency is a very common snag, and it slows us down from growing in our view of God. Naturally, if we're not in the Bible, we cannot know the God of the Bible.

The best way to move forward toward consistency is to start small and doable—something like a two-week Bible reading plan that will take you five to ten minutes a day. There are loads of free apps out there that have these small plans. I also have several in my online shop (katieorr.me/shop). Get the quick win and build on that success. Place your energies on consistently showing up.

This doesn't mean that you won't learn anything—you will—but you need to first put your best effort toward getting into a rhythm of regularly opening your Bible, even when it feels confusing or "not enough."

Tips for building the habit

Start over tomorrow. Look at your schedule and decide on a time and place you will read. It could be on your lunch break, right before you go to bed, or after you get out of the shower. Feel free to experiment with finding a good time. (And when you find yourself forgetting to open your Bible and it's been a few days, head right back here: Start over tomorrow.)

Make it enjoyable. Grab a new coffee mug or some yummy hot chocolate reserved only for your time with God. Buy a new blanket to cozy up with, or a pretty basket to keep your Bible and accessories in. I like to keep a few napkins (in case I spill my coffee) and sticky notes handy in my basket, along with a pen in case I need to jot down something I need to remember to do later.

Find a trigger. What do you do most days without fail? Brush your teeth? Take your lunch break? Drink your morning cup of coffee? It is easier to establish a regular rhythm of Bible study if we can find a way to attach our time in the Word to an activity that is already fairly set in our schedules.

When I do _____ I will read my Bible.

Before I do _____ I will do my Bible study.

After I finish _____ then I will open the Word.

As soon as you finish brushing your teeth, open your Bible to read for five minutes. Bring your Bible with you to lunch, or open up a Bible reading app to enjoy alongside your chicken salad. Brew your coffee, then pore over the Word of God as you sip on that cup of joe. Fill in the blanks above with possibilities and try them on for size until you find what fits in this stage of life.

Invite a friend to read the same plan, and consider meeting up in a week or two to talk through what you've read. Knowing others are on this journey with you is a powerful encouragement to keep going. (If you can't think of anyone to invite to join you, consider an online group. I have a community you can join at biblestudyhub.com.)

Keep going. Don't give in to the paralysis of perfectionism, which says, "If I can't do it right, then I shouldn't do it at all." Resist the thought that reading for five minutes isn't good enough. If you were given a bite-sized version of your favorite candy bar, would you reject it because it isn't a king-sized bar? No! You would take and enjoy it. Take what you can get today. Enjoy it. Then show up tomorrow and do it again. Five minutes of Bible reading is always better than zero.

Pray for a desire to be in the Bible. As you move forward and make the daily choice to know God better through the Word, ask Him to give you more and more of a craving for His Word. It is His will for you to love the Bible. Pray toward that end.

Manage your expectations. Don't get bogged down with the way so-and-so does it. Figure out what works for you, and don't expect to be running right away. Be patient with yourself. You are not a baby giraffe.

Gain Understanding

> Like newborn infants, desire the pure milk of the word, so that you may grow up into your salvation, if you have tasted that the Lord is good.
>
> 1 Peter 2:2–3

> Do your best to present yourself to God as one approved, a worker who has no need to be ashamed, rightly handling the word of truth.
>
> 2 Timothy 2:15 ESV

We all start out as a Bible study beginner. Peter encouraged the Christ-followers under his care to be like babes who long for the milk that will enable us to grow up. Our spiritual life is just like our physical life. In order to grow, we must take in nourishment. The rate of our spiritual growth is in direct correlation to the amount of "milk" we take in.

No Bible, no growth. A little bit of Bible, a little bit of growth.

Though we all start out as beginners, there is an expectation that we grow in the skill of Bible study. There is a biblical expectation that every believer, over time, ought to be able to open the Bible, read it, study it, figure out what it means (interpret it), and walk forward in worship of the God who wrote it (apply it). All Christians should eventually be able to pick up a fork and knife and dive in to a dinner of the Word for themselves.

> Although by this time you ought to be teachers, you need someone to teach you the basic principles of God's revelation again. You need milk, not solid food. Now everyone who lives on milk is inexperienced with the message about righteousness, because he is an infant. But solid food is for the mature.
>
> Hebrews 5:12–14

If my fourteen-year-old was still being spoon-fed puréed vegetables, everyone could recognize that there is a problem with his growth. Yet there are many who are decades old in the faith and either still living off Bible baby food (devotionals) or not regularly eating at all. This is not meant to be a guilt trip. It's meant to be a reality check. We need to take a good, hard look at our ability to read and understand the Bible so that we can correctly assess what our next best step is. The spiritual diet of every Christian should eventually move from milk to meat.

Tips for gaining understanding

Ask the right questions. Most of us tend to approach the Bible asking two questions: "What does this mean to me?" and "What am I supposed to do?" These questions are not in and of themselves bad questions to ask, but they ought not be asked first. As we've already chatted a bit about, the best question to ask is always, "What do I learn about God in this passage?" Not every verse holds a truth about God, but the Bible is the Word of God. It is the special revelation about God, from God, from which we can know Him better. The first thing on our minds when reading and studying the Bible ought to be to learn more about who God is.

Get a good study Bible. This might be the best initial investment you can make in your spiritual life. Filled with helpful notes, charts, maps, and more, a good study Bible will help you understand the main teachings of each passage as well as the big picture themes of the Bible. (I share all about my favorite study Bible at katieorr.me/fav.)

Know the context. Your new study Bible will be a big help with this. Or you can use free online tools to learn more about what I refer to as the "three A's": author, audience, and aim. Author: Who wrote the verses you are reading? Audience: Who was he writing to? What was going on with them at the time? Aim: Why did he write it? What did he hope to accomplish through writing it? We cannot know what the Bible means to us until we know what it meant to them, the writer and audience of the text.

Learn a few study methods. We all learn differently, so what works for me may not work for you. But look for a method that helps you slow down and digest what you are reading. There are four pillars to any good study method: read, observe, interpret, and apply. Over time, our Bible study efforts will be most fruitful if we include each step. I have several e-courses you can go through that teach you more about these pillars. Head to katieorr.me/basics to get my basic Bible study class for free.

Be patient. I've been studying the Bible seriously for over two decades and there is still much for me to learn. I am frequently having "aha" moments in the Word of God. But every one of the aha's have been preceded by months, if not years, of study. Keep going. It's worth it.

Ask for help. Utilize your local church. Phone a friend. Google it. Be an active learner when you don't have a clue what you are reading. I guarantee you are not the first to have the questions you're asking.

Remember why you're studying. This is not a goal to achieve or a status to reach. This is all about knowing God better and enjoying all He's provided for us. We study the Bible to grow closer to God and live out the Happy Soul realities He's already given us.

Pray. Every time you sit down to read the Bible, pray and ask God to lead you and help you. My favorite prayer for this is found in Psalm 119:18 (ESV): "Open my eyes, that I may behold wondrous things out of your law."

Remember. Remember. Remember.

The Bible is filled with the command to remember. Often it is an explicit and obvious statement. But just as much, if not more, there is an implicit suggestion to remember. Take the Ten Commandments, for example. They are filled with "do this" and "don't do that," but when we read them, we typically miss what is at the beginning of these commands: "I am the Lord your God, who brought you out of the land of Egypt, out of the place of slavery" (Exodus 20:2).

Before God instructs them, He recalls to the mind of the listener that He is their rescuer. Do you remember the story of the Exodus? This is when God delivered the Israelites after four hundred years of slavery to the Egyptians. They had been enslaved, with no future and no hope for change, until God sent them a deliverer—Moses—to stand up to Pharaoh and rescue them from bondage. God exhibited power over nature through the plagues and parting seas, then proved His ultimate rule over all nations through defeating Pharaoh and his army. It's as if He is saying, "Do you remember all I did for you? Do you recall how in awe of me you were when I delivered you? Do you remember the power I displayed over nature and nations? I am in control. I am King. And I am offering you a new way to live. Follow me."

We see this pattern in the New Testament as well. Perhaps most obvious is in the book of Ephesians. The first three chapters of this book are filled with truths about who God is and all He's done for us. It's not until chapter 3 that Paul gets into all the details of the "do's and don'ts." However, there is one command tucked away in the first part of Ephesians. Want to guess what it is? Yep, it's *remember*. Again and again, Scripture calls us to remember. Remember what you've been saved from. Remember who you are now. Remember what I've done for you. Remember how much I love you.

Remember. Remember. Remember.

The goal is not to simply know right things about God. Nor is it simply to try harder. The end goal is worship. And as we choose to look for God on the pages of Scripture and rightly respond to who He is, we take our first steps toward becoming a Happy Soul. The most important thing about us is what we believe about God.

And as we believe better—as our view of God becomes more and more accurate—our lives will be transformed by who He is.

So today, if you are feeling especially unhappy, perhaps a good dose of remembrance will do you a load of good. Remember who God is. Remember who you were before meeting Christ. Remember all He's done for you. Remember all He says about His love for you. Remember all the good plans He has for you. Even when our circumstances tell us something different. Even when we are feeling unhappy. Even when the unthinkable happens. The Happy Soul remembers that God is good and near and gracious and in-control. Always.

Remember. Remember. Remember.

Tips for remembering

Create a truth journal. Grab a spiral-bound book of 3x5 cards or a small journal you can fit in your purse or pocket. Look up verses that pertain to the area you are struggling with the most—especially those verses that remind you about the character of God and all He has promised us. Paralyzed with anxiety? Look up verses about God as your provider. Afraid of the future? Write out passages that teach about God's sovereignty. Dealing with guilt? Cling to the verses that tell of God's forgiveness. Write them out in your journal. Keep the notebook handy throughout the day. Add to it as you encounter additional verses that remind you of who God is. Praise God for who He is and ask Him to conform your thought-life to the truth of who He is.

Hang truth on your walls. I love Scripture art that I can hang in my home. They are continual reminders of His character and love for me and my family. Beyond decor, you can write out truth (perhaps some of the same in your truth journal) on a 3x5 card and tape it to the mirror in your bathroom, or stick it somewhere on the dashboard of your car, or put it in a sandwich baggie and tape it up in your shower. Post reminders wherever you spend a lot of time, as continual reminders of who God is.

Sing Scripture. Find albums that put Bible verses to music, or worship songs that help set your mind on who God is. Music is a powerful tool to help us remember the goodness of our God.

Hide His Word. Perhaps the best way we can remember the amazing character of God is to place those truths where no one can snatch them away. Bible memorization is one of the most fruitful endeavors we can spend time and energy on. When temptation strikes, it is the best weapon we can have, to have His Word stored in our minds and engraved on our hearts. Pick one verse you need to remember most of all. Make it *your* verse. It may take a while to learn it, but start hiding those truths in your heart today.

As we continue on the path to better Bible study through building the habit and gaining understanding, and as we choose to remember what we've learned to be true about God—as we believe better— more and more of our moments will become Happier ones.

> Who do I have in heaven but you?
> And I desire nothing on earth but you.
> My flesh and my heart may fail,
> but God is the strength of my heart,
> my portion forever.
>
> Psalm 73:25–26

> You give him blessings forever;
> you cheer him with joy in your presence.
>
> Psalm 21:6

> But I will see your face in righteousness;
> when I awake, I will be satisfied with your presence.
>
> Psalm 17:15

SOUL SEARCHING

Happy Soul Evaluation

Answer the following by circling where you are in your Happy Soul journey.

Do I have a tendency toward a self-centered or God-centered reading of the Bible?

1   2   3   4   5   6   7   8   9   10
Self-centered   *God-centered*

When I find myself in difficult seasons, do I tend to grab at God's Word as a security blanket—a collection of comforts—or do I cling to it as my lifeline?

1   2   3   4   5   6   7   8   9   10
Collection of comforts   *My lifeline through the storm*

How do I typically measure spiritual growth?

1   2   3   4   5   6   7   8   9   10
A change in behavior   *A growing view of God*

Where do I tend to put my energies most?

1   2   3   4   5   6   7   8   9   10
Trying harder   *Believing better*

Where am I in my journey to better Bible study?

1   2   3   4   5   6   7   8   9   10
Bible study beginner   *Able to teach others*

1   2   3   4   5   6   7   8   9   10
No desire for the Bible   *Can't get enough of it*

1   2   3   4   5   6   7   8   9   10
No idea what the Bible is about   *Consistently growing in my knowledge of the Word*

Now that you've taken an honest inventory of where you are, circle with a different colored pen, or underline, where you want to be for each. Spend some time in prayer, and ask God to make these changes in your life.

Happy Soul Action

Take the next step in your Bible study journey.

If you are not currently in the habit of regular Bible study, decide when and where you will spend time with God through the Bible tomorrow. Pick out a quick and easy reading plan and gather everything you'll need for that time.

If you are ready to move from Bible reading to studying, check out the free e-course I mentioned before, at katieorr.me/basics, or ask some friends what they use to study the Bible. Start trying out different study methods to help you grow in your understanding of the Bible.

Consider at least one action step from the "Tips for Remembering" suggestions a few pages back.

Happy Soul Prayer

God, uncover my self-centeredness, self-reliance, and pride. I confess my lack of love for your Word. Grant me a deep desire for time in the Bible. Help me understand it. Open my eyes to see you more clearly through what I read. I long to know you better and enjoy your presence in my everyday moments. I need you to change my focus. Help me take my eyes off of myself, my problems, and my pain. Instead, I choose to fix my gaze on you. I want to enjoy your presence more and more.

SECRET #2

THE HAPPY SOUL
IS RESOLVED
TO FOLLOW
GOD'S WAY

6

Resolved

The LORD is good and upright;
therefore he shows sinners the way.

Psalm 25:8

My degree is in medical technology. It's a bit of an obscure field and has actually been renamed since I graduated. Essentially, it's lab work. If you've had your blood drawn or peed in a cup to have it sent off to the lab, it comes to us. Analyzing your specimen is what we specialize in.

Right out of college I worked full time in a huge hospital. My time was split between the chemistry lab and the blood bank. I enjoyed the blood bank so much more because it was all manual work, whereas chemistry was mostly run by machines. I also had a very competent co-worker in the blood bank (we'll call her Lucy). She already had tons of experience, and since I was the newbie, that was a great comfort to me. The blood bank is serious business. When a patient needed a blood transfusion, we received the orders for a type and cross-match. We would figure out what blood type the patient is (A+, B-, etc.), select compatible bags of blood, then continue further testing to ensure there would be no life-threatening incompatibility reactions. Yeah, so the whole "this patient will die if you mess this up" pressure was real. Thus, why I *really* liked working with competent, experienced Lucy.

On the nights where we didn't have many orders to fill, I would attempt to get to know Lucy a bit through small talk. I learned that she had been in the military, liked to read, and wasn't originally from Florida, but that was about all I could get out of her. As time went on, I could tell she would rather be lost in her book than talk to me, so I defaulted to bringing something to keep me occupied for those slow evening shifts. Since that part of the lab was small, I often would move into our supervisor's office to read, as our boss had previously told me I was welcome to use the space on her desk if needed.

After we had worked several months together, I noticed Lucy had progressively become more quiet—even grumpy—around me. She was impatient with my newbie questions about work, and stuck to as little interaction as possible. I could tell something was up.

One evening, after months of tense work shifts, as I was quietly reading at our supervisor's desk, Lucy stormed in and lit into me about being disrespectful to our supervisor, about how inappropriate it was that I sat at her desk night after night. Lucy proceeded to tell me how much trouble she would have been in if she did that while in the military—this was utterly despicable behavior. Then she went back into her shell in the opposite corner of the laboratory to read her book by the plasma freezer and returned to acting as if I didn't exist.

Well, then.

Looking back, her growing displeasure in my attempts at small talk make a whole lot of sense now. She spoke to me only when necessary to get our job done because she was utterly annoyed by my presence and couldn't stand to be in the same room as me! I was a constant offense to her protocol.

She was furious. I was frustrated. Needless to say, our work hours together from there on out were frigid.

Maybe you too have had a situation where you could tell you've offended someone but you didn't know exactly what you did wrong. You had been held unfairly to an unspoken code of conduct— leaving you in a continual state of violation in their eyes. This is a very frustrating and hopeless place to be.

God Has Clearly Communicated to Us through the Bible

Gratefully, this is the exact opposite of what is true of our God. He has not left us in the dark. His Word has given us very clear directions for most areas of our lives.

At the heart of the Psalms is this truth, that God's Word brings us light, direction, hope, and life. Thus, we can declare with the Psalmist that "Your word is a lamp for my feet and a light on my path" (Psalm 119:105).

God has been so good to us to give us instructions, and you and I have much more than the Old Testament to go off of. We now have the full counsel of God's perfect Word at our fingertips. Not only that, but we live in an age of information in which commentaries and many other Bible study tools are easily accessible to us. We have no excuse for not knowing who God is and what He desires for His people—from how we spend our money, conduct our days, and handle our thought-life, to how we worship, talk to, and tell others about Him. The will of God has been made clear to us in the pages of Scripture. Each command is for our good. Every truth is there to light our way.

This is not to say that understanding everything in the Bible is easy. It's not. But it is available, accessible, and approachable. God is not a distant, grumpy co-worker grumbling behind our back about how offended He is by our actions. He is a clear communicator, a gracious guide, and a merciful master who has given us objective, explicit instructions on how to know and follow Him.

Therefore, the Happy Soul is resolved to follow God's Way.

The Grace-Filled Agreement God Made with His People

> All the LORD's ways show faithful love and truth
> to those who keep his covenant and decrees.
>
> Psalm 25:10

For much of my early Christian life, I saw the Old Testament as a random collection of really weird and obsolete commands. I didn't understand the beauty and specificity of it, nor did I get why it was so important. This disregard toward the Old Testament slowly eroded my view of the New Testament, and therefore all of what was taught in the Bible. I've come to see that understanding the Old Testament is critical to our understanding of the New Testament. They are different parts of the same story.

The Bible is essentially the story of God making himself known to His people. Time and time again we see God interrupting life as they knew it in order to introduce himself to them. From Noah to Abraham to Moses, we see people who knew little to nothing about God, and with each encounter, God revealed more of who He was. This theme is throughout all of the Bible and is called God's progressive revelation: Over time, He has progressively revealed more and more to us about who He is and what He has planned. Though we don't know with complete clarity everything that is to come, we know today more about God and His plans than the people of Jesus' day. That early church who gathered after Jesus' death and resurrection understood more than the nation of Israel during the time of King David. Those kingdom people knew more about the first tribes of the sons of Israel, who knew more about God than Noah and His sons.

You get the picture.

Alongside this progressive revelation of who God is and all He has planned, is the thread of the covenant. The covenant is an agreement—a treaty—made between God and His people. There are several specific covenants made, but each one is an agreement that built on the one before it. The covenant God made through Moses is perhaps the one you've heard most about. It included the Ten Commandments and was followed with a ton of details (recorded in Deuteronomy and Leviticus) for what following those commands would look like in the everyday life of an Israelite.

> All of you are standing today before the LORD your God . . . so that you may enter into the covenant of the LORD your God, which he is making with you today, so that you may enter into his oath and so that he may establish you today as his people and he may be your God.
>
> Deuteronomy 29:10, 12–13

This covenant agreement made between God and His people was not a random list of oddball rules. It followed a common type of treaty during that time. God entered into the customs and culture of His people—He spoke their emotional language—in order to communicate His commitment and love to them. Treaties were a normal part of life for these ancient people. Treaties provided safety and security based on the power and provision of the one whom they made an agreement with.

> I will turn to you, make you fruitful and multiply you, and confirm
> my covenant with you. . . . I will walk among you and be your God,
> and you will be my people.
>
> Leviticus 26:9, 12

God committed to providing for and protecting His covenant people. He alone would be their salvation, and the expectation was that they would "observe the words of this covenant and follow them, so that you will succeed in everything you do" (Deuteronomy 29:9). They would forsake all other gods and follow God's way. And His way was not arbitrary. It was designed to protect and provide for both the individual and the community. Following His Way preserved God's holy presence among them. Following this special Way of God also proclaimed to the nations around them that they were God's people.

God is still providing safety and security for His people. And following God's Way is still what leads to an enjoyment of God's best plan for His people. "All Scripture is inspired by God, and is profitable for teaching, for rebuking, for correcting, for training in righteousness, so that the man of God may be complete, equipped for every good work" (2 Timothy 3:16–17). If we want to live the complete, prosperous life of a Happy Soul, we have to have the truths of God's Way settled in our hearts and minds.

God is good and gives instructions for our good.

Following His Way leads us into the protection, provision, and presence of God.

God's protection, provision, and presence leads to our flourishing.

Therefore, if we want to flourish, His Way is to be fully followed.

The Happy Soul is resolved to follow God's Way.

The Need for Careful and Complete Following

My middle child, Anna, loves to bake. At first she started out with boxed mixes for cupcakes and cookies, with great success. She has a collection of cookbooks for kids, gifted to her by generous grandparents. Over time, she's grown braver in her choice of recipes, and she began to try out several from-scratch cake recipes. However, for quite a while, attempt after attempt flopped.

After seeing (and tasting) the final product of several recipes, I began to do some investigating. When I asked some questions, I began to realize that she didn't quite understand the importance of using exact ingredients and specific measurements. In one very interesting chocolate cake recipe, she found that we were out of vanilla extract, so she added lemon flavoring instead. In another cupcake attempt, since she couldn't find any baking soda, she used baking powder. Others flopped because measurements were not double-checked and either received too much or too little of an important ingredient.

It was time for an intervention. We started with a chat about chemistry—because baking is essentially chemistry. You can't just throw a few things together and hope it comes out okay. Baking requires you to carefully follow the instructions in order to implement the formula, adding ingredients with specificity (no substitutions!) and measuring them with accuracy. If we want good cookies, we need to follow the good instructions.

Likewise, even though we are Happy in name, our external experience often does not match our internal status, and if we want our internal identity to match our external reality, we need to follow the recipe. God's Word tells us how. This is not a family recipe that is kept under lock and key to guard the proprietary formula. God's recipe for a Happy Soul is clearly communicated through the pages of Scripture. It is filled with good instructions and is meant to be followed carefully and fully. But before we can get to the how-to's, we have to have it settled in our soul that instructions are a good thing.

Recipes are created for a reason.

The Happy Soul is resolved to follow the recipe of God.

Discovering God's Way

> How happy is the one who does not
> walk in the advice of the wicked
> or stand in the pathway with sinners
> or sit in the company of mockers!
>
> Psalm 1:1

If we want to follow the recipe, we need to know what it is. The first few lines in Psalm 1 give us what the Happy Soul *doesn't* do. And although these words aren't super prescriptive, they are descriptive: The Happy Soul lives her life with intentionality. She is determined to walk a certain way. But in case we need a clearer picture, we are given just that in Proverbs from wise King Solomon.

> Happy is a man who finds wisdom
> and who acquires understanding,
> for she is more profitable than silver,
> and her revenue is better than gold.
> She is more precious than jewels;
> nothing you desire can equal her.
> Long life is in her right hand;
> in her left, riches and honor.
> Her ways are pleasant,
> and all her paths, peaceful.

> She is a tree of life to those who embrace her,
> and those who hold on to her are happy.
>
> Proverbs 3:13–18

Here we have another "Happy sandwich" with the use of our Happy Hebrew word אַשְׁרֵי ("ash-ray") at the beginning of verse 13 and the end of verse 18. It is a descriptive portrait passage, just like Psalm 1. Here, the Happy Soul finds/acquires wisdom and understanding, which is personified as Lady Wisdom. Wisdom is stated to be the best investment and the greatest treasure one can find. She will bring abundance and contentment. Holding tight to her leads to the tree of life, which is symbolically used here to point to eternal life.

The poetry of both these passages points us toward an intentional progression. Each progression brings a greater commitment. In Psalm 1 there is the progressive refusal to walk, stand, or sit in the way of the wicked. Conversely, here in Proverbs 3 we see the positive and active progression of following God's Way: She acquires, treasures, and embraces wisdom.

The Happy Soul acquires the recipe.

The Happy Soul treasures this recipe.

The Happy Soul embraces the recipe.

Then the Happy Soul is resolved to follow it.

Acquire the recipe

For the LORD gives wisdom; from his mouth come knowledge and understanding.

> Proverbs 2:6

Perhaps you've heard a bit about Solomon's story. The son of King David (the one who, as a very young man, defeated Goliath with his slingshot and a few stones), Solomon inherited the kingdom of God's people after King David's death. Early in his reign, God appeared to Solomon and offered to grant him one request. Here is Solomon's reply: "Lord my God, you have now made your servant king in my father David's place. Yet I am just a youth with no experience in leadership. Your servant is among your people you have chosen, a people too many to be numbered or counted. So give your servant a receptive heart to judge your people and to discern between good and evil. For who is able to judge this great people of yours?" (1 Kings 3:7–9).

Solomon asked for a receptive heart and discernment so he could hear from God and lead God's covenant people to follow the way of God. God answered by giving Solomon "wisdom, very great insight, and understanding as vast as the sand on the seashore" (1 Kings 4:29).

Heart-level wisdom, insight, and understanding from God—this is what Solomon asked for and this is what he received. This was more than just worldly wisdom. This was seeing the world through God's eyes as much as one earthly man could.

Where can we get this wisdom and understanding today? Just like Solomon did—from God himself. We already hold God's insight in our hands. It is spelled out in the pages of Scripture. And though we may physically possess a copy of the Bible, we may not yet have acquired wisdom. The true acquisition of God's wisdom comes with the consumption of God's Word. "For the word of God is living and effective and sharper than any double-edged sword, penetrating as far as the separation of soul and spirit, joints and marrow. It is able to judge the thoughts and intentions of the heart" (Hebrews 4:12). This is exactly what Solomon desired when he asked God for a receptive and discerning heart, and it is what we have been given in God's Word to us.

The Happy Soul is resolved to follow God's Way.

First she must learn to truly acquire it.

Then she must treasure it.

Treasure the recipe

> Follow my advice, my son;
> always treasure my commands.
> Obey my commands and live!
>
> Proverbs 7:1–2 (NLT)

Once Chris and I were engaged, I began to pay a bit more attention to the couples in our church. I wondered how long they'd been married, what their wedding was like, and where they had met. Suddenly there was this new demographic of people whom I knew very little about but about whom I wanted to know as much as I could. I remember one couple in their thirties who often sat in front of us on Sunday mornings. I don't know exactly how old they were, but judging by the way they dressed, my guess is they graduated high school in the late '80s. From hairstyles to color choices, they seemed stuck in that decade.

Here's where you get a peek into my petty thoughts. I couldn't fathom why someone would *not* want to keep up with the trends. How could someone be satisfied wearing a decades-old dress or a sweater that screams 1989? Fast-forward several months: We got married, purchased our first house together, and suddenly I got it. The money I frivolously spent as a single woman seeking to be a fashionista now had a new purpose: home equity. Now, I am not saying that every single woman is frivolous with her money, nor am I saying that all married women are more frugal. I am only saying that this was true of me, and owning a home gave me a new direction for how to spend my money.

About two years later, after we had our first child, what I treasured was turned upside down one more time. Once again, I saw that my spending was not as smart as it could be. I had decorated walls to death and filled our rooms with furniture under the guise of upping the value of our home. However, with this new bundle of joy in my arms, keeping a human being alive seemed like a much better way to spend our limited income.

With each change, I had to ask myself, What do I value most? Staying in style? Investing in our home? Feeding and diapering and clothing our child? And with each rung of greater responsibility came a deeper love and higher treasure. What I treasured ultimately dictated how I acted. The Happy Soul sees God's Word as a great treasure, and thus will invest in the pursuit of gaining wisdom and understanding.

So often the Bible and its teaching is portrayed as irrelevant and old-fashioned, restrictive and unattainable. God's Way is not something to be endured or begrudgingly followed. It is the way to a Happy Soul life. Time in God's Word is the best investment we can make. Wisdom from God's Word is the greatest treasure we can find, because God's wisdom teaches us God's Way, and following God's Way is how we stay close to God himself. But God's Word is timeless and always relevant because the reality of our heart's need for rescue and guidance is the same as it has always been. Even more so, the character of the God who provided the protection of His Way is the same as it has always been.

We must stop listening to the voices that tell us the Bible is irrelevant and out of date. We must quit following the whims of the culture that promises satisfaction in another gadget, accomplishment, or a new relationship. These can bring a temporary feeling of happiness, but ultimately leave us unsatisfied and longing for more. It is not bad to pursue those things, but we must recognize they ought to never be what we treasure the most. Our greatest possession—the one that brings satisfaction, joy, contentment, and delight—is that of the Bible, which spells out how to know and follow God. And it is through knowing and following God that we experience all our soul longs for.

> You reveal the path of life to me;
> in your presence is abundant joy;
> at your right hand are eternal pleasures.
>
> Psalm 16:11

The Happy Soul is resolved to follow God's Way. She acquires it, treasures it, and then she embraces it.

Embrace the recipe

> Hold on to instruction; don't let go.
> Guard it, for it is your life.
>
> Proverbs 4:13

I love my wedding band and engagement ring. But they both have a series of channel-set diamonds that don't get the attention they deserve. My fabulous mother-in-law faithfully cleans her ring nightly. My ring cleaning, however, is random and sporadic. A couple years ago, during one of my on-a-whim cleanings, I was working on getting the gunk out of the crevices of the channel, but something wasn't quite right. The more I cleaned, I noticed that one of the diamonds seemed a bit loose. After a slight push with my fingernail, it fell out entirely. Then another did. And another. After a moment of freaking out, I grabbed each of those tiny, precious diamonds and the rest of the set and placed them in the middle of my palm. Then I squeezed my fist shut as tightly as I could, covered that fist with my other hand, and headed straight to the kitchen drawer where we kept our sandwich baggies. I carefully placed the loose diamonds and the toothless ring into a double-sealed bag. Then I sealed that bag within another double-sealed bag. I was determined not to lose even one quarter of a carat.

Why go to such lengths to protect those small stones? Because that ring is precious to me. My husband, then boyfriend, worked hours and hours, many moons ago, to save up for our engagement. So when I received his gift, I quickly became hypervigilant when it came to my ring. It is a symbol of the covenant we made with one another. Not only is it precious to me emotionally and spiritually, but it is monetarily valuable. I rarely take it off. It has become such a part of me that there is an indentation around my fourth finger where my ring lies. If I don't have it on, I feel naked.

God's Word is meant to be part of us in such a way. We ought to cling to God's Way so closely that we are permanently marked by it. It becomes such a big part of our regular rhythms and future planning that we cannot live without His direction, His wisdom, His instructions. Following God's Way is a precious and irreplaceable source of joy. Without the Way of God, we would be lost. I'll admit, I do not always hold on to God's Way with the same fervency and careful attention as I did those diamonds.

Our God is a gracious God, who showers His people with abundant lovingkindness through the protection and plan He gives us through His Word, in order to preserve His presence in our daily lives. His directions to us are not random. Nor are they ancillary to our lives as believers. They are designed for us to flourish. They are the way to the satisfaction and delight we crave; therefore, we must choose intentionality and obedience to God's Way. This necessity of intentional efforts by the Happy Soul is made plain in Scripture. The current of the culture we live in runs opposite from the direction we are called to. Thus, we are swimming upstream and it takes persistent effort fueled by the Holy Spirit in order to keep moving toward God.

Remember, there is a progression here. One leads to the other until they all become the same pursuit: following God with everything we have. This is not an easy road. It's a narrow one. It's a disciplined one. But it is a rewarding one.

> So get rid of all the filth and evil in your lives, and humbly accept the word God has planted in your hearts, for it has the power to save your souls. But don't just listen to God's word. You must do what it says. Otherwise, you are only fooling yourselves. For if you listen to the word and don't obey, it is like glancing at your face in a mirror. You see yourself, walk away, and forget what you look like. But if you look carefully into the perfect law that sets you free, and if you do what it says and don't forget what you heard, then God will bless you for doing it.
>
> James 1:21–25 NLT

> Your word is a lamp to my feet
> and a light to my path.
>
> Psalm 119:105 ESV

> Enter through the narrow gate. For the gate is wide and the road broad that leads to destruction, and there are many who go through it. How narrow is the gate and difficult the road that leads to life, and few find it.
>
> Matthew 7:13–14

> Thus says the Lord:
> "Stand by the roads, and look,
> and ask for the ancient paths,
> where the good way is; and walk in it,
> and find rest for your souls."
>
> Jeremiah 6:16 ESV

7

Grasp God's Way

I am sure of this, that he who started a good work in you will carry it on to completion until the day of Christ Jesus.

Philippians 1:6

Understanding the Need for Personal Involvement

In college I took a ton of chemistry classes, all of which were accompanied by regular laboratory time. We put into practice the theory we were learning from the lectures at that time. Chemical reactions copied down in our notebooks were later physically carried out in a beaker. Many experiments included a catalyst. Without the catalyst, the reaction would still occur . . . eventually. With all the components present, the final product would be produced, but the addition of a catalytic agent greatly sped up the rate of the reaction.

So it is with our spiritual growth. Ultimately, our transformation into a Happy Soul is a work of God, yet we have a catalytic role to play in that work. Just like those chemical reactions carried out in the lab, all the necessary components for spiritual transformation are present. All those who have put their faith in the work of Christ on the cross will be made to look just like Him . . . eventually. It is the certain work God has started, is working, and will complete within us. That is the equation. We are the catalysts.

Remember our "already but not yet" status we chatted through in part 1? We are already saved, but not yet. We are already a Happy Soul, but not yet. God has made us into a Happy Soul as part of our new identity in Christ (justification). God is making us into a Happy Soul as we partner with Him to work out that reality (sanctification). God will make us into a Happy Soul when we see Him face-to-face and the work He has begun in us is completed (glorification). It is then, in heaven with Christ, we will enjoy and worship God forever without the presence of sin. And though we will never experience the perfect presence of our holy God on this side of eternity, we can certainly begin to get a glimpse of it. The transformation has begun. But the extent to which we see that metamorphosis realized here on earth is affected by our participation in or neglect of following God's Way.

You and I are the catalysts of change in our own spiritual lives. The believers who understand their role of obedient choices as a catalytic agent will experience this transformation more quickly and more fully. Those who rarely engage in this work will see the bulk of their transformation occur on the other side of this life where God's work of salvation will come to completion. I want to be as close as possible to what God has planned. Don't you?

The first step to following God's Way is understanding that He has crafted His Way to include you and me. His Way utilizes the actions of His people.

So what does this catalytic work actually look like? We cannot play our part if we don't know what that part is. There are thousands of commands in the Bible, but they all boil down to this: Love God with all we have. When asked about God's Way and which command is greatest, Jesus replied, "Love the Lord your God with all your heart, with all your soul, and with all your mind. This is the greatest and most important command. The second is like it: Love your neighbor as yourself" (Matthew 22:37–39). This love for God is an active, obedient love, as "whoever keeps his word, truly in him the love of God is made complete" (1 John 2:5).

To love God is to obey God. To obey God is to love God.

I think, deep down, we already know this. We cannot say we love God if we don't at least attempt to walk in His way. I could spend time here listing out all the "rules and regulations" of following Christ, but that would miss the point. The end goal of God's Way is not to simply follow the rules. God's Way is given to us so that those who love Him can enjoy His holy presence. Let's take a look at a few "next best steps" to take in our pursuit of loving and obeying God.

> Jesus answered, "If anyone loves me, he will keep my word. My Father will love him, and we will come to him and make our home with him."
>
> John 14:23

Read the Bible for yourself

My husband loves Diet Pepsi. I love Dr Pepper. Every once in a while, our drinks get mixed up at a restaurant and I can often tell the drink in front of me is not what I ordered before I even take a sip. They smell different. But when I taste it, I can immediately identify the sweet sugar of Dr Pepper or the metallic taste of aspartame. Even though diet sodas are attempting to replace regular sodas, the difference is obvious to anyone who enjoys the real thing. If someone had never tasted either, they wouldn't know whose drink was whose.

You and I need to know the true message of God so well that we can spot a fake immediately. Don't take everything a Christian speaker teaches at face value. Study it for yourself. Don't blindly read books labeled as Christian—including this one! Check out the context of the verses used. If the book doesn't include many verses, don't take their main points as absolute without being sure it lines up with Scripture. Let's be women who are influenced and filled by God's Word rather than a message filled with some words about God.

As you move forward in personally knowing what the Bible says, consider the views you hold: your actions and speech, the way you spend your time and money, what you believe about parenting, marriage, and sexuality. Do you hold to a particular view because one of your favorite bloggers does? Are you holding tight to a specific way of parenting or praying because you heard someone talk about it? Examine the conversations you hear and the teachings you have received through the lens of what the Bible says. You very well might end up back where you started from, in that position, but now you'll know why you believe it and where (and if) the Bible teaches on that topic.

We Christians are really good at making a mess of things. In particular, those on the conservative end of things tend to make that which is gray in the Bible a rigid black and white. Those on the progressive side of things tend to muddle and mess with that which is already very clear in Scripture.

Both are dangerous. Both hinder our ability to grasp God's Way.

The only way for you to know when something is being taken too far in either direction is for you to know God's Word for yourself. Study it. Dwell on it. Pray it. Live it. Love it.

> Teach me, LORD, the meaning of your statutes,
> and I will always keep them.
> Help me understand your instruction,
> and I will obey it
> and follow it with all my heart.
>
> Psalm 119:33–34

Seek out the sages

That being said, we still need the voices of mentors in our spiritual lives. From both modern and historical spiritual guides, we have piles of books and files of resources at our fingertips to help us know God's Way. The Bible is a deep work of art, and it will take some coaching and expertise to enjoy its fullness. The physical writing of this book took several months, but the research for this book took no fewer than two years of biblical study and the reading of fifteen books by experts to help shape my teaching. This doesn't mean that you need to spend two years on something before you can apply what you are learning, but it is always a good idea to seek out the expert opinions of biblical scholars who know what they are talking about.

Beyond the literary world, look for people in your own backyard to seek out. I hope you are a part of the local church. I hope your pastor preaches God's Word more than his own opinions. I hope there are women in your local church with whom you can talk about what you are learning. A spiritual helper doesn't have to be a biblical scholar; she can be only a few steps ahead of you in her own walk with God. Pray and ask God to show you someone to reach out to. If you aren't in a church that is teaching the Word of God, find a new one. If you are in between churches, listen to sermons online (check out their beliefs page first) while you eagerly await your new church home. Keep seeking the wisdom of those who have been theologically trained to help you know and love the Bible.

> Help me understand
> the meaning of your precepts
> so that I can meditate on your wonders.
>
> Psalm 119:27

Invest in your spiritual life

> Blessed are those who hunger and thirst for righteousness, for they will be filled.
>
> Matthew 5:6

My friends Shannon and Lori are Happy Souls. I've been able to watch their lives over the past year in a unique way as we've met weekly to study God's Word and discuss how to follow God's Way. They are busy women. Yet they faithfully show up week after week for our discipleship group having completed their studies and Scripture memory work for the week. I never have to remind them to show up or to study. From day one they've taken ownership of their commitment to know God better through our time together this year.

My friend Delaney is a Happy Soul. She has seven children. Her oldest is twelve, and her youngest is just several weeks old. Yet this doesn't keep her from attending church. She is unwilling to let her life circumstances be an excuse for disobedience. Delaney is resolved to follow God's Way to be an integral part of a local church.

My friend Bonnie is a Happy Soul. She studies God's Word as seriously as anyone I know—even comparable to those who have been to seminary. She's part of the senior generation that sometimes struggles with technology, but she has learned to make it work for her so she can study and teach the Word of God better to her Sunday morning small group. She doesn't make excuses, she doesn't sneer at change, she doesn't put her preferences over others' needs. Bonnie is committed to using her retirement years to follow God with everything she has.

My friend Lara is a Happy Soul. She's walked through a rocky marriage yet clings to God's Way. She's refused to give in to the temptations of bitterness and revenge. Instead, she has sought reconciliation and love again and again. She's listened intently to God's voice through over a decade of pain. She's held fast to that which is black and white in the Bible, and sought God's direction in the gray. She's pursued and submitted to the leadership of her local church for wisdom and guidance. Through the safety net of God's Word and God's people, she has navigated the choppy waters of her marriage.

My sister Sarah is a Happy Soul. As a young wife and mom, she's stared cancer—and all the scary what-ifs—in the face with confidence in God's sovereignty and power, His good plan, and abundant grace. Pity and despair had no hold on her. Fear and anger did not paralyze her. She pressed on through treatments and surgeries (all while homeschooling six kids) with the peace that surpasses understanding. Her faith did not waver because her foundation of who God is is firm.

I know hundreds of other Happy Souls. They are men and women who have chosen to invest in their spiritual life. A significant portion of their time and resources is spent toward knowing and obeying God's Word. Because of these investments, they are experiencing the fruit of His presence. Their lives are not perfect. They've all walked or are walking through some sort of tragedy, heartache, trial, or betrayal. Yet even when their circumstances are hard, their heart is full. Even when they *feel* unhappy, their internal reality is that of unexplainable peace and overflowing joy.

We've chatted a lot about knowing and esteeming God's Way, but the reality is, if we don't *actually* act on it, we are not *actually* following it.

God's Way Leads to Our Flourishing—An Example

I attended private schools from preschool through high school. All of those private schools were faith-based schools—both Protestant and Catholic. I've been around God's Word all my life. I've heard all the do's and don'ts. Most of what I was taught boiled down to individual actions—a laundry list of sins to avoid. But what I didn't understand was that those individual pieces were part of a beautiful whole. Those individual actions were more about the promised outcome than the particular moment. I thought God wanted me to seek perfection, when what He really wants is for me to seek Him. I thought sin was to be avoided because it was simply bad to be in sin. *Don't drink, don't have sex, don't tell a lie. These things are bad.* Yet the real problem with sin is not just the sin itself. The real issue is that sin hinders my relationship with God. As long as I hold on to sin, my intimacy with God is hindered.

I can see this clearly played out in my journey through romantic relationships. When I first came to Christ, nothing much changed for me, in practice. I felt better about myself, like I had done something right in God's eyes to "get saved." I also had a new certainty for where I would spend eternity. But externally, not much about me changed. Through my private school teaching and youth group attendance, I had gathered a nice list of do's and don'ts when it came to relationships with guys: Be careful not to wear provocative clothing, don't put yourself in compromising situations, and definitely don't have sex. I didn't question these suggestions, but I never understood the *why* behind it all. I didn't know that God's Word taught about His good plan for our hearts, our relationships, and our sexual activity. I didn't know that marriage and sex were created by God and are for His glory. The do's and don'ts of "Christian dating" were given, but they were given without the context of a good God with a good plan.

I had yet to learn about waiting on God's perfect timing. Nor did I understand how much He loves me and wants what's best for me. I didn't understand that the parameters He had set for sex were for my good. I didn't realize the connection with the heart and body, and how God—who created every nerve ending and body part—created sex to facilitate the bond between man and wife. I was taught to avoid sex in order to avoid an STD or a teen pregnancy. And I was not taught that, more than anything, the consequences of sin is distance from God. As a young woman, I wanted connection more than anything. I wanted to be seen as desirable, and I sought the significance of having a boyfriend, being liked, and seen as beautiful.

As I began to take my faith in God seriously, receive teaching through sermons and small groups, and studied the Bible for myself, I was able to see a better way. A way that was not primarily about avoiding the bad, but pursuing the good. A life that leaned in and trusted God—a good, all-knowing, all-loving God—who always had my best in mind.

Over time, my relationships changed as I knew God better. I quit manipulating situations to find myself in a relationship. I quit throwing around kisses and became more interested in what God thought of me than what the guys did. I realized that my significance and worth could never be found in an earthly relationship.

I learned that I didn't have to take matters into my own hands. Instead, I could wait on the God who knows my future. I started following God's Way not just to avoid the consequences, but in order to stay close to Him. I became more focused on God and His Word than I did on who was attractive and available.

This led to a fruitful season of singleness. The desire to be loved and connected was still there, but it no longer controlled me. I found that God's love brought a sense of significance I could never find in a man. And after several years, I found myself in the first relationship done God's Way. We set physical boundaries that were far, far away from the line of sin, not because we were supposed to, but because we wanted to love and honor God through our time together. I kept my heart in the moment instead of always longing for more. I stayed in the Word and didn't allow my relationship with a guy to overshadow my relationship with God. After about a year of dating, we broke up. But there were no regrets. Only good memories. Both of us met and married our current spouses within a few years of our breakup, and we were able to walk forward into these new relationships even more confident in God's good plan for our individual lives. We had each grown closer to God from our time together. God's Way led to our flourishing!

I have loads of other stories, short and long, from all different areas of my life that point to the goodness of following God's Way. I've seen it enough in my own life to say this with great confidence: Following God's Way is pursuing our happiness. To pursue happiness is to follow God's Way.

What to Do When We've Messed It All Up

Perhaps you are feeling that all this talk of following God's Way is unrealistic or too hard. You might even look at your life and feel as if you have messed up way too much to ever get it right. Here's the good news: There is always mercy and grace for our mess-ups.

You and I can start following God's Way at any moment, in any situation, even if we are running headlong the opposite way. *Yes,* there are still consequences for our sin. *Yes,* this world is sin-stained and broken. But we are never too far from God's reach. For the Happy Soul, there are no limits to His mercy; there is no exhausting His grace. Gratefully, we always have the choice to repent and return to following His Way.

> As he was saying these things, a woman from the crowd raised her voice and said to him, "Blessed is the womb that bore you and the one who nursed you!"
>
> He said, "Rather, blessed are those who hear the word of God and keep it."
>
> Luke 11:27–28

SOUL SEARCHING

Happy Soul Evaluation

How do I view God's Word?
(*Circle on the scale the way you most often act toward God's commands.*)

1   2   3   4   5   6   7   8   9   10
Something I regularly pass up   *Indispensable instruction*

Am I resolved to follow God's Way, or am I attempting to create my own recipe?

1   2   3   4   5   6   7   8   9   10
My way is best   *God's Way is best*

How active am I in my own spiritual growth?

1   2   3   4   5   6   7   8   9   10
Not trying to grow at all   *Moment-by-moment partnering
with God*

Am I actively investing in my spiritual life?

1   2   3   4   5   6   7   8   9   10
I am hesitant to spend my resources   *All I have is His to use*

Happy Soul Actions

Try out a new Bible study method this week.

Pay attention to who God has planted around you. If you are not already part of a local church, start looking for one right away. If you are already part of a church, look for potential sages. Get to know them. Express your desire to learn more about how to follow God. Ask her what has been fruitful in her own walk with God.

Invest in your spiritual life. Look at your time, money, and other resources. Continue to set aside time to meet with God. Look into purchasing a good study Bible or other resource that will help you comprehend God's Way better.

Happy Soul Prayer

God, I am so grateful for your instruction! You are so good to give me clear directions on how to love and follow you. Give me a greater love and gratitude for your Word. When there is hesitation to walk in obedience, grant me the grace needed to take the next step toward your holy presence. Where there is ignorance, bring enlightenment. As I stumble, light my path with your precepts. Help me to embrace the purpose of holy living. I long to glorify you with all that I have and all that I am.

SECRET #3

THE HAPPY SOUL
IS ATTACHED
TO GOD'S WORD

8

Attached

How happy is the one who does not
walk in the advice of the wicked
or stand in the pathway with sinners
or sit in the company of mockers!
Instead, his delight is in the Lord*'s instruction,*
and he meditates on it day and night.

Psalm 1:1–2

Until college, religious private school was all I knew. I grew up around both Protestant and Catholic teachings as part of my education. I learned the typical Bible stories (David, Jonah, Abraham, Joseph, etc.), a bit about the life of Jesus, and I knew how to find Leviticus or 2 Thessalonians before anyone else in a Bible drill. I went through First Confession and First Communion in second grade. I don't remember too much about either of those, besides that all the kids were impressed if you could walk up to the priest with an open mouth, instead of open hands, to receive the crisp communion wafers. I certainly didn't understand the heart behind the stories and disciplines I was taught in any of the schools I attended. Prayer, confession, and the rest of the Christian practices were yet another task to complete in my quest of becoming the best.

Though I knew a lot *about* the Bible, I didn't know how to *use* and *enjoy* God's Word. The Bible was yet another book in my locker: World History, Geometry, Biology, Holy Bible. It didn't come home with me unless I needed it to study for a test or wanted to brush up on my speed drill skills. The Bible was simply a source of yet another A on my report card. It was surely not something I treasured. If I had realized the life-giving power it contained and the truths within it that told me who I already was because of Christ, I may have spared myself years of fruitless pursuit of that which would never satisfy. Had I known that the Bible is God's words to me and the way to know and enjoy Him, I would have studied it with fervor. Instead, it remained a list of do's and don'ts and a telling of archaic stories that I thought had nothing to do with my everyday living.

If the Happy Soul is resolved to follow God's Way, then this next secret is a logical next step. In order to follow God's Way with all we have, then we need to love the Bible. However, this is not the reality for most. Instead of being a source of delight, the Bible is often a source of guilt and confusion. It feels more like eating a bunch of boiled spinach than it does our favorite bowl of ice cream. Instead of experiencing feelings of joy, excitement, and fulfillment when opening the Bible, many of us experience the following feelings:

Judgment
Condemnation
Sadness

Unworthiness

Shame

Guilt

Confusion

Frustration

Boredom

Inadequacy

Houston, we have a problem. How on earth can we acquire, treasure, and embrace the Way of God spelled out in the Word of God if we are overwhelmed with all these negative emotions surrounding the Bible? Perhaps this is not the case for you. Maybe you open your Bible faithfully and joyfully every day. If so, way to go! You've mastered this secret. But for the rest of us who struggle to open the Bible and find it hard to *love it with everything we are*, this section is for us. There is a deep connection between loving God's Word and following God's Way; we will never be mature Christ-followers if we don't have a strong attachment to His Word.

Do you remember in chapter 1 when we chatted about the covenant? This was the treaty God made with His people where He initiated mankind. Through this initiation, God gave His special people specific instructions on how to know, serve, and ultimately worship Him. When they spoke of God's Word to them, their list was very different from the list I made above. In fact, we have a list of theirs preserved; it is found in the poem of Psalm 119. This Psalm is an intentionally crafted series of declarations about God's Word. "It is a pattern, a thing done like embroidery, stitch by stitch, through long, quiet hours, for love of the subject and for the delight in leisurely disciplined craftsmanship."[1] From this poetry we get a very different sense of God's Word.

Delight
Exceeding love
Wonderful
Life-giving
Sweeter than honey
Better than gold and silver
Pure, true, trustworthy, righteous, endures forever
Brings light, peace, strength, joy, understanding, comfort, and
    pleasure

Throughout the psalm we also see declarations made—resolutions by God's people in regard to their relationship with God's Word.

I cling to them
I trust in them
I have studied them
I am overcome with longing for them
I will never forget them
I will follow them with all my heart
I will not wander from them
They are my meditation, my heritage, my treasure, my lamp,
    my light, my counselors, my hope, the joy of my heart, and
    the theme of my song.

A few years ago I was invited to speak at a women's conference in my hometown in Southern California. Since my family relocated to Alabama a few weeks after I graduated from high school, it had been decades since I'd been in that town. I arrived a bit early to visit with family, catch coffee with a few high school friends, and wander around my old stomping grounds. It was an extremely emotional trip for me as I remembered the girl who grew up in that town and all God has done for her since then.

The conference was hosted at a church just a few miles from where I attended high school. During the break on Saturday, I drove my rental car over to the school campus so I could walk around campus a bit. It's a small private school, and it was basically the same as I remembered it, with a few additions. The same small chapel stood where I used to hear God's Word taught every Friday. The same beige lockers lined the outdoor hall of the high school wing. The same left-behind sweaters, assignments, and notebooks were strewn about, cluttering the hall. As I walked the hall, smiling as the memories flooded over me, one locker stopped me in my tracks.

On top of that locker was a Bible.

Scribbled on and dog-eared.

Pages torn and spine destroyed.

Abandoned until Monday.

Awaiting to be flippantly thrown into a backpack and brought to Bible class.

It looked just like mine had when I was there. It was being treated just like mine had been. And, most likely, the owner of that Bible lacks a love for their Bible just as I did. For so long I saw the Bible as just another textbook. A chore. A roadblock. A burden of guilt. As I type, I am weeping at the memory—that I ever had such a casual distain for the Word of God, that I forfeited so much time with Him and took on so much trouble without Him when I could have been enjoying the benefits of being a Happy Soul. Deep down, I had been renamed a Happy Soul. I could feel it. I knew there had to be something more but I had no idea how to obtain it. I didn't know how to enact change. My view of God was off. I could follow the do's and don'ts, but I didn't know how to get closer to God himself. And I certainly didn't love God's Word.

We've all been there, haven't we? Perhaps you are there right now. Your Bible may not be as physically neglected as the one I saw that Saturday afternoon, but it is neglected nonetheless. It gathers dust on a shelf, sits on the floorboard of your car throughout the week, or is lost somewhere in your bedroom. Or perhaps you are opening your Bible but are just going through the motions. You read. You check "read Bible" off your list. You close your Bible. You keep walking. There's no attachment to the Word of God. No true closeness to God. There's no awe and wonder. There's no overwhelming love and feelings of delight. You'd rather be enjoying the next Netflix episode or clinging to your Facebook feed instead of spending time with God through His Word.

The Happy Soul Delights in God's Word

> For in my inner self I delight in God's law.
>
> Romans 7:22

> Your words were found, and I ate them.
> Your words became a delight to me
> and the joy of my heart,
> for I bear your name,
> Lord God of Armies.
>
> Jeremiah 15:16

For me, one huge reason why there was no attachment to the Bible was that it scared me. I didn't understand it. I didn't like some of what I had read. I certainly didn't understand that it was God's very words to me. I thought it was an archaic system of rules and a weird collection of stories. I didn't see the beauty of

God's Word. I didn't understand the purpose of His revelation to us. I didn't see that the Bible was a gift of grace, not a list of laws.

As we clearly see in Psalm 119, God's people *loved* God's words to them. They saw the Law as a great gift of grace! It was a treasure! It was a much needed black and white description of how they should act and react to one another, as well as how to know and worship God. Before God made himself known, ancient people wandered in their attempts to know the divine. There were hundreds of gods out there whom they could choose to follow and worship. But not one of these gods spoke. Not one of them was personal.

> Their God has chosen to reveal himself and to tell them plainly what he expected of them. . . . In the Old Testament the Israelites are not heard complaining about the burdensomeness of the law. It was a great example of God's love for them that he would communicate to them in this way. . . . The law is viewed as a delight rather than drudgery, as freedom of Revelation rather than fetters of restriction.[2]

Though our lives are very far removed from the way of ancient life, perhaps we could benefit greatly from their perspective. They loved God's Word—it was life-giving to them—because it was clear and specific, personal and provisional.

Most of us don't have a delighting problem. We delight in and enjoy many things just fine. God has created us for pleasure. Just think about it. God created our bodies to enjoy things! Eating food is primarily about keeping ourselves alive, yet we've been given taste buds and a variety of sweet and savory food to eat. Functionally speaking, sex is about keeping the human race going, yet God has wired male and female bodies to enjoy one another. There is no room for doubt: God created us to experience deep delight.

This enjoyment doesn't stop at physical pleasures. From BFFs to family, to the children in our lives, we are also created to emotionally enjoy each other's presence. God gives us good gifts to enjoy. But we need to train our hearts to delight in the right things and in the right amounts. Unfortunately, we're really good at delighting in counterfeits that will never satisfy.

When it comes to our emotional thirsts, there are loads of counterfeits out there that promise to satisfy us in ways only the Word of God can. But they always leave us hankering. Every soul is emotionally thirsty and hungry. We all have a longing for more. Sometimes we just don't recognize what that longing really is. We search for satisfaction in so many other things: a deeper relationship, a bigger promotion, a higher accolade . . . but they ultimately leave us empty. They are counterfeits of the real thing.

Jesus made this clear in a conversation with the Samaritan woman at the well. We don't know her name, but we know that Jesus saw her at the well and knew her emptiness. It is likely that she'd been mistreated and cast aside most of her life. As Jesus pursued her broken heart, he chatted with her about the well water: "Everyone who drinks from this water will get thirsty again. But whoever drinks from the water that I will give him will never get thirsty again. In fact, the water I will give him will become a well of water springing up in him for eternal life" (John 4:13–14). Not long after this encounter, while addressing the crowds of people, Jesus claimed, "I am the bread of life . . . No one who comes to me will ever be hungry, and no one who believes in me will ever be thirsty again" (John 6:35). Jesus taught that only He could satisfy our deepest desires. And the Bible shows us how to come to Jesus with our cravings. "If anyone thirsts, let him come to me and drink. Whoever believes in me, as the Scripture has said, 'Out of his heart will flow rivers of living water'" (John 7:37–38 ESV).

Our salvation brings a quenching to our soul that we will enjoy for eternity. But as we pursue to work out our salvation—as we resolve to make our internal identity become an external reality—we have to keep drawing from the well of the Word, which grants us the way to the One who can satisfy our souls. God's Word gives us perspective, instructions, and parameters needed to navigate this sin-stained world. It is our protection. Our hope. Our guide. Our grace.

> I have your decrees as a heritage forever;
> indeed, they are the joy of my heart.
> I am resolved to obey your statutes
> to the very end.
>
> Psalm 119:111–112

The Happy Soul Meditates on God's Word

> How I love your instruction!
> It is my meditation all day long.
>
> Psalm 119:97

The word *meditation* in our modern context conjures up thoughts of yoga pants and breathing techniques. This is not what was meant by the author, nor is it what the original audience would have thought of. The original Hebrew word translated here as "meditation" holds the meaning to mutter, utter, roar, and talk. It is the idea of a slow mulling over, a continual processing, a personal musing. This same Hebrew word is used in Psalm 2 when "the peoples plot." Ever mutter anything under your breath? That utterance is a verbal overflow of what you are meditating on. It is in this sense that we are encouraged to meditate on the contents of God's Word.

What we talk about often reveals what is on our minds. When we are planning our next vacation or working on a big project, most of us can't help but talk about it. When something affects us emotionally either for good or bad, it is evidenced in our speech, because what we plot and plan is often what we talk about. What we mull over and meditate on will eventually be on our lips. "For the mouth speaks from the overflow of the heart" (Matthew 12:34).

I'm a verbal processor, so for me this reality cannot be more true! What my mind is set on is what I need to talk about. The talking is connected to the thinking, and the thinking to the talking. In fact, in preparation for writing this book, I intentionally taught through Psalm 1 when I could. It was fruitful to process what I'd been studying through verbal communication. My poor husband has heard more about this book than he probably cares to admit. Because it's been on my mind. It's been my meditation. And so, it's been on my lips.

> This book of instruction must not depart from your mouth; you are to meditate on it day and night so that you may carefully observe everything written in it.
>
> Joshua 1:8

Here we see a meditation progression: Meditation leads to action. Meditate on the Word *so that* you can carefully follow it. The Happy Soul has the Word of God in a mental crockpot. And this deep mulling over and intentional plotting through Scripture leads to the fruitful, abundant, Happy Soul life we desire. It's not enough to simply hear the Bible; we must ingest it, think about it, process it, talk about it, keep it with us mentally day and night. This rumination changes us.

In Matthew, Jesus told another parable to help us understand the importance of receiving the Word in this meditative way. After his telling of the parable, he then explains exactly what he meant by it.

> So listen to the parable of the sower: When anyone hears the word about the kingdom and doesn't understand it, the evil one comes and snatches away what was sown in his heart. This is the one sown along the path. And the one sown on rocky ground—this is one who hears the word and immediately receives it with joy. But he has no root and is short-lived. When distress or persecution comes because of the word, immediately he falls away. Now the one sown among the thorns—this is one who hears the word, but the worries of this age and the deceitfulness of wealth choke the word, and it becomes unfruitful. But the one sown on the good ground—this is one who hears and understands the word, who does produce fruit and yields: some a hundred, some sixty, some thirty times what was sown.
>
> Matthew 13:18–23

The parable speaks of four types of hearers:

1. The one who hears but does not understand (v. 19)
2. The one who hears, has an emotional response to it, but it doesn't take root—proven by lack of roots (vv. 20–21)
3. The one who hears but does not receive it (v. 22)
4. The one who hears and understands—proven by abundant fruit (v. 23)

My guess is you have people in your life who listen but don't hear, or hear but don't understand. Oftentimes as a mom I feel like a broken record. I give out the same instructions and warnings daily. I have one child in particular who is a horrible listener. Though my child is not deaf, my child definitely has a hearing

135

problem. My words seem to go in one ear and out the other. There is a difference between *hearing* the physical sounds coming out of my mouth and *understanding* what I am saying. Other times, it may be that my child hears my words but they don't take root, or my child chooses not to receive it. Over time, I've begun to require my kids to say "yes, ma'am" once they hear my instruction, or else ask for clarification if they don't understand what I'm asking them to do. Together, we've defined "yes, ma'am" as "I hear you and I intend to obey." This communicates to me that they aren't merely hearing me, but they also understand my instructions.

This passage is *not* teaching that just because someone doesn't understand everything in the Bible, that they are not saved. It *is* teaching that there is a receiving of the Word that goes beyond a mere nod to the facts or a quick emotive response to a sermon. The hearing exhibited by person #4—the hearer who also understands—includes both an intellectual and emotional piece. The hearing leads to a deep recognition of their need for Christ—one that leads them to throw themselves on the mercy of God. The immersive, meditative, intellectual receiving of what the Word teaches will always lead to transformative action. The proof of true-hearing is in the fruit-bearing.

Additionally, this hearing and understanding of what God has to say to us ought not stop at the moment of salvation. Just like the first leaves of a sprout are a simple showing of more to come, so ought the initial fruit evidenced by the understanding of the Word be the first of many shows of our salvation. This fruitful Happy Soul is passionately attached to God's Word. She delights in God's Word because she knows it is the only way to the flourishing life. She meditates on God's Word. Meditation enables her delighting. Delight fuels her meditation.

"Therefore, everyone who hears these words of mine and acts on them will be like a wise man who built his house on the rock. The rain fell, the rivers rose, and the winds blew and pounded that house. Yet it didn't collapse, because its foundation was on the rock. But everyone who hears these words of mine and doesn't act on them will be like a foolish man who built his house on the sand. The rain fell, the rivers rose, the winds blew and pounded that house, and it collapsed. It collapsed with a great crash."

Matthew 7:24–27

9

Enjoy God's Word

How sweet your word is to my task—
sweeter than honey in my mouth.

Psalm 119:103

Becoming deeply united to God's Word, through delight and meditation, is a lifelong journey. Often we need to take a step back and look at our reality before we can move forward. I suggest a three-pronged approach to moving toward enjoying God's Word more and more each day: probe, preach, and pray.

Probe—Look for the Barriers that Hinder Our Hearts from Enjoying God's Word

So how do we move forward? How do we go from feelings of condemnation and confusion to dedication and delight? How do we change our heart's posture from seeing the Bible as a boring chore toward that of a life-giving pleasure? We need to figure out what is holding us back. There are two barriers we often face when it comes to enjoying our time in the Bible and therefore treasuring it more and more.

Look out for lies

Many of our barriers boil down to lies.

I'm not a reader.

I'm not smart enough.

I'm not spiritual enough.

I'm not disciplined enough.

Each of these lies assume that some Christians are naturally bent toward loving God's Word without effort. The rest are simply stuck in a subpar spiritual existence. I still believe this lie sometimes. I admire the spiritual rock star who seems to have an endless knowledge of the Bible. She consistently rises at 5:00 a.m. to enjoy a deep time in the Bible. She seems to make all the right choices. Then I start to compare my own measly spiritual existence. I am not an early riser. I don't understand all the passages. And I don't always follow God's Way.

She is a spiritual superstar. I am a spiritual failure.

Lies, lies, lies. Yes, those spiritual rock stars may be further down the road than I am, but it is not because they have some sort of superpower I don't have. They have made choices. They have invested in their spiritual life. They have decided that if they want to know God better and follow His Way, they *desperately need* God's Word. Over time and with great intentionality, I'm getting there: to the place that recognizes that I too desperately need God's Word. I want to know God better and better each day. I want to follow Him in obedience through walking in His Way. So I open my Bible, and the more I do it, the more I love it. So much so, that my desire for God's Word has led me to do crazy things such as listening to extra sermons throughout the week, placing Scripture art throughout my house, buying music that is Word-based so I can enjoy it on the go, spending hours working on my Bible memory work, setting my schedule around time in the Bible, and buying books that help me understand God's Word better. I have chosen to invest my time, my money, my energy, and my affections on the Word of God. And the reward of God's presence leads me to crave His Word more and more and more.

If you are believing the falsehoods that you are not smart enough or spiritual enough or disciplined enough, I implore you to recognize them as lies and kick them to the curb! They are not your friends. They are your excuses. They are your enemies. And they are not doing you any favors. Make the choice to move forward and invest in your spiritual life through opening the Word of God. The more you do, the more you'll find your attachment growing. Because if you want to be a Happy Soul, if you want to have a clearer view of who God is, if you want to be the obedient Christian, and (most important) if you want to enjoy the presence of God more and more each day, you must love the Bible.

Let go of independence

Another barrier to growing an attachment to God's Word is a lack of necessity. We simply don't think we need the Bible in our lives every day. We think we can live without it. We believe we can thrive on our own.

Before the age of modern plumbing, cisterns were often used where a well could not be dug. The house we lived in in Kentucky had a cistern. It was under the front porch and was once the primary source of water for the house. Rainwater was gathered and funneled into the large concrete holding tank. At some point before we lived there, that cistern broke. It could no longer hold water. With the cracks in the cistern came the introduction of dirt and critters. Our downstairs bedroom backed up to the cistern and we could hear them scurrying around at night. I can't even imagine the nastiness that is in there. Years of muck lay at the bottom of that tank.

> For my people have done two evil things:
> They have abandoned me—
> the fountain of living water.
> And they have dug for themselves cracked cisterns
> that can hold no water at all!
>
> Jeremiah 2:13 NLT

This is the reality of a broken cistern. This is the nasty picture of trying to live life our own way. Instead of delighting in all God has provided for us, we try to store up our own supplies. Instead of planting ourselves deeply into the life-giving streams of water God offers, we trudge along and attempt to scrape together a vessel to collect water on our own. Yet our efforts can never keep the water we need. Our vessel only collects the mud and junk and who-knows-what at the bottom . . . while the water we desperately need escapes us.

If we want to enjoy the overflowing life God has created us to enjoy, we must recognize that any effort made to create our own replenishments will always be cracked and incomplete. There is only one way to spiritual flourishing: God's Way. And God's Way is found in God's Word. Therefore, the Happy Soul recognizes that she needs to be rooted in the streams of God's Word. This leads to a genuine attachment to God's Word.

Instead of a source of judgment, the Happy Soul sees the Bible as her source of the good life.

Instead of a boring book of bedtime stories, the Happy Soul recognizes that opening her Bible is spending time with the God of the universe.

Instead of a pursuit she'll put off until she has more free time and mental energy, the Happy Soul sees the Bible as her indispensable lifeline to God.

Preach—Fight for the Inclinations of Your Heart

> Happy are those who keep his decrees
> and seek him with all their heart.
>
> Psalm 119:2

> So, you too consider yourselves dead to sin and alive to God in Christ Jesus.
>
> Romans 6:11

Do you remember when I introduced you to Old Katie? Although Old Katie is no longer who I really am, she's still around. The Bible calls our old selves the flesh. It's the part of us that is bound by sin, which God is rescuing us from. This is why the apostle Paul says in Galatians 2:20, "I have been crucified with Christ, and I no longer live, but Christ lives in me." Earlier in Romans, we learn that this was all "so that we may no longer be enslaved to sin" (Romans 6:6). The part of me that loves to sin has been dealt a mortal blow. It is dead, but it is still dangerous.[1]

Because of this reality, our hearts are continually in a conflicted space. In this "already but not yet" life we live, there is a moment-by-moment battle for the throne of our hearts, which is why we see so many commands in Scripture to lay aside, put to death, and put off the old self.[2] The war within our souls is a critical one for us to engage. Our old self—though it has been dealt a mortal blow through the death and resurrection of Christ—will run rampant within us if we don't put it in its place. We fight this battle by preaching. We tell ourselves again and again what is true about

143

us because of Jesus. We remember who we really are. Old Katie isn't going down without a fight.

> For I know that nothing good lives in me, that is, in my flesh. For the desire to do what is good is with me, but there is no ability to do it. For I do not do the good that I want to do, but I practice the evil that I do not want to do. Now if I do what I do not want, I am no longer the one that does it, but it is the sin that lives in me. So I discover this law: When I want to do what is good, evil is present with me. For in my inner self I delight in God's law, but I see a different law in the parts of my body, waging war against the law of my mind and taking me prisoner to the law of sin in the parts of my body.
>
> Romans 7:18–23

Here Paul gives an honest accounting of the state of his soul. It is conflicted. He recognizes that his "flesh" (Old Paul) has nothing good within it. It is driven by evil desires and attempts to take him captive. Yet he also states that his "inner self" delights in God's law. Deep down, New Paul loves God's Word. Deep down, New Katie loves God's Word. Deep down, New You loves God's Word, too. We need to learn how to listen to and unleash our inner self—the part of you that already loves God's Word. We need to tell our old selves to take a hike.

> Take off your former way of life, the old self that is corrupted by deceitful desires, to be renewed in the spirit of your minds, and to put on the new self, the one created according to God's likeness in righteousness and purity of the truth.
>
> Ephesians 4:22–24

Pay attention to the voices you are listening to. There are a million things vying for our attention, both internally and externally. The external battle can be engaged with choices and boundaries, but the internal fight is much different. If you're anything like me, it's my own voice that I hear the most. Quit telling yourself the Bible is boring. Stop saying that you are not smart enough to enjoy God's Word. Preach to yourself what is true in Scripture. Tell your soul how it is. Declare with the psalmist that you treasure God's Word.

> I rejoice in the way revealed by your decrees
> as much as in all riches.
> I will meditate on your precepts
> and think about your ways.
> I will delight in your statutes;
> I will not forget your word.
>
> Psalm 119:14–16

> I have treasured your word in my heart
> so that I may not sin against you.
>
> Psalm 119:11

Pray—Ask God to Do What Only He Can Do

Ask, and it will be given to you. Seek, and you will find. Knock, and the door will be opened to you. For everyone who asks receives, and the one who seeks finds, and to the one who knocks, the door will be opened. Who among you, if his son asks him for bread, will give him a stone? Or if he asks for a fish, will give him a snake? If you then, who are evil, know how to give good gifts to your children, how much more will your Father in heaven give good things to those who ask him.

> Matthew 7:7–11

There are a lot of times when I *want to want to* read my Bible. I *want to want to* make better choices. I *want to want to* love and honor God with all that I am and all that I have. But wishing for a deeper love for God and His Word won't carry me very far. I need something stronger than a momentary desire for change. I need to engage my inner self—the part of me that truly delights in the Bible. She's always there. But she's often shoved down and silenced.

Beyond probing—paying attention to the barriers that keep us from enjoying God's Word—and preaching to ourselves, we also need to pray. The best way for our inner self to come out and play is to call her out with prayer. We've already seen in Romans 7 that deep down, our inner selves love God's Word, even if we *feel* we don't. If we are in Christ, we have a new heart and new desires. Paul often prays for the hearts of God's people, as we see here in Ephesians 3:16: "I pray that he may grant you, according to the riches of his glory, to be strengthened with power in your inner being through his Spirit." In this same letter, Paul tells us that this inner being, our new self, is "created according to God's likeness in righteousness and purity of the truth" (4:24). Through Christ, we already have an inner being—a Happy Soul—that loves God's Word and longs to follow God's Way.

It's important that we pray for others, but we must also pray for ourselves. Not just for traveling mercies and better sleep. Not just for the job promotion and the alleviation of symptoms. We need to be eagerly praying for our inner Happy Soul to emerge more and more from her cocoon. We have been reborn. We are Happy Souls who have been made righteous by God and who love God's Word. We need to do the work of prayer to uncover her.

This is the confidence we have before him: If we ask anything according to his will, he hears us. And if we know that he hears whatever we ask, we know that we have what we have asked of him.

1 John 5:14–15

This is a pivotal passage when it comes to our prayers. It is God's will for us to love His Word and follow His Way. If we ask God to increase our love for His Word and the ability to follow His Way, He hears us. If we know that He hears the prayers of His people that are according to His will, we know that He will answer those prayers. Not only that, but the very Spirit of God "helps us in our weakness" when it comes to our prayers, and "intercedes for the saints according to the will of God" (Romans 8:26–27). You can enjoy God's Word.

So much about becoming a Happy Soul hinges around the Word. So if you are in a place where you don't desire His Word—probe, preach, and pray! Pray with confidence for your desire for the Word to increase. Ask God to change your heart. Ask Him to show you how to make time with Him a priority. Pray the following passages back to God. Ask Him to make these words true of your own heart.

> Help me stay on the path of your commands,
> for I take pleasure in it.
> Turn my heart to your decrees
> and not to dishonest profit.
> Turn my eyes
> from looking at what is worthless;
> give me life in your ways.
>
> Psalm 119:35–37

> I have sought you with all my heart;
> don't let me wander from your commands.
> I have treasured your word in my heart
> so that I may not sin against you.
>
> Psalm 119:10–11

> I find my delight in your commands,
> which I love.

147

I will lift up my hands toward your commands, which I
    love,
and will meditate on your statutes.

                                   Psalm 119:47–48

Your testimonies are my delight
and my counselors.

                    Psalm 119:24

How I long for your precepts!
Give me life through your righteousness.

                         Psalm 119:40

SOUL SEARCHING

Happy Soul Evaluation

How much do I look forward to spending time in the Bible?

1........2........3........4........5........6........7........8........9........10
I dread it   I love it

Happy Soul Actions

PROBE

Spend some time journaling out your current feelings about God's Word. Don't sugarcoat it!

_____

_____

_____

_____

_____

_____

Take a good, hard look at what keeps you from opening your Bible. Write out all the barriers you can see.

_____

_____

_____

_____

_____

PREACH

Identify any lies you may believe about yourself and God's Word. Tell your soul what to believe. Below are a few examples.

God's Word is what I really need.
I love God.
I want to follow Him.
I cannot afford to go without regular time in the Bible.
I am not too busy.
God has given me everything I need to live a godly life.
I can and will enjoy God's Word.

_____

_____

_____

_____

_____

PRAY

Pray through the verses on pages 147–148. Speak them out loud. Write them out. Ask God to make those verses the reality of every part of your soul.

_____

_____

_____

_____

_____

Happy Soul Prayer

God, I do love your Word! Help me love it more and more each day. Show me what I am engaged in that is smothering my love for your Word. Uncover the sin that hinders my desire for you and your Way. I want my everyday reality to be that of the psalmist who is desperate for your Word. Help me take the next step today to enjoy time in your Word.

THE HAPPY SOUL IS DEPENDENT ON GOD'S PROVISION

10

Dependent

God, you are my God; I eagerly seek you.
I thirst for you;
my body faints for you
in a land that is dry, desolate,
and without water.

Psalm 63:1

It is remarkable how quickly most of us have become dependent on our smartphones. Depending on how old you are, you may know nothing different. If you are my age (forty-one at the release of this book) or older, you certainly remember life before smartphones. In college, none of my friends had a cell phone; we had to make plans ahead of time to meet up with each other. There was no texting to say we would be late. No pulling up GPS directions on the go. We had to think carefully through the next day's plan and get ready for it the night before. However, there were also no worries about getting full bars in order to check email and no incessant searching for a power outlet.

We now live in a digital society, and staying constantly connected is part of the norm. But in order to stay connected and in order to have full access to all the benefits our smartphones can provide, we have to keep plugging into a power source. If our smartphones are dead, they are useless. So we charge our devices every night, or else our next day will be severely hindered. Because if you are like me, so much of my life is lived on my phone—my calendar, my pictures, my work, my communication with the ones I love are all done throughout the day on my phone. Keeping my smartphone charged is always a high priority. It is with this same consistency and fervency we must plug in to God's power for our spiritual life.

God is our unfailing source of life. He is the well that will never dry up. The stream that forever flows and is filled with living water—the only type that brings vitality to our souls. It is never stagnant or polluted. When our roots are deep down in the streams of His presence, we experience an abundant, prosperous, Happy Soul life that is independent of circumstances. We obtain a soul-satisfaction that is solely dependent on the presence of His sustenance.

> He is like a tree planted beside flowing streams
> that bears its fruit in its season
> and whose leaf does not wither.
> Whatever he does prospers.
>
> Psalm 1:3

Several winters ago I got to visit Fairbanks, Alaska. It was in the dead of winter, but the scenery was stunning—and very different from the Florida "winter" landscape! I especially noticed that there are trees that are never seen in Florida: beautiful bare birch trees and lots of unique evergreens. One of my favorites—with their dark green color, towering height, and slender form—was the spruce trees. They were everywhere. And super tall! The Sitka spruce, Alaska's state tree, can grow up to 225 feet tall and live to be seven hundred years old!

As my friend Rachel graciously drove me around town to see all the sights, she pointed out a patch of spruce trees that looked to be a cute family of new baby trees—not very tall, but just as pretty as all the momma trees behind them. However, Rachel pointed out that these trees, which looked to be baby trees, were actually not babies at all. They were adult trees that found themselves planted in permafrost, which is soil that never fully thaws out. Though the permafrost is below the surface, it negatively affects the soil quality above it—it acts as a blockade to the roots of the trees. Therefore, their potential for growth is severely stunted. Those pretty spruce trees will be babies forever.

Unfortunately, this is the state of way too many Christians today. Spiritually speaking, they are chronologically older than their external maturity shows. Some have been Christians for decades but are babies in their faith. Instead of being thoroughly entrenched in the nourishment they need, they are spiritually stunted for lack of roots. That was me. It was years after the moment of salvation, before I ever started *really* growing. And before I did, though I was several years older, I didn't look much different from when I first came to Christ.

A weak, shallow root system leads to a superficial faith.

A strong, anchored root system leads to a vibrant faith.

Shallow sips produce scanty roots.

Deep drinks provide a broad base.

Too often we focus our energy and activity on looking good. We want to look like a good Christian more than we want the goodness and presence of Christ. We want others to think we have it all together while we ignore the only power that can keep us thriving. When we put all our efforts toward the *appearance* of growth instead of working toward developing a deep root system, we set ourselves up for an anemic and stunted spiritual life.

For way too long I was satisfied with shallow sips in the stream of God's stores. I thought I could do things on my own. I didn't really need God . . . and when I did feel the need for Him, I didn't really know how to "put down roots." I wasn't deeply rooted. I wasn't plugged in. I was flying solo. There are still times when I forget to plug in to all God has provided for me. I wander away from my source of power. I believe I can get by without a charge and I'm left absolutely depleted. Instead of being a well-watered tree with an extensive root system, I've all too often been like the Alaska spruce trees stuck in permafrost, shallow and stunted.

If you and I want to grow and develop into a strong, beautiful believer, we too must become tenaciously embedded into all God has provided for us. In the next chapter, we are going to look at the details of what being deeply attached looks like, practically speaking. But first, I want us to look at all we have to look forward to by being firmly fixed to God's power and grace, because the Happy Soul is dependent on God, and this affects everything about her.

The Happy Soul Is Fruitful

> He is like a tree planted beside flowing streams
> that bears its fruit in its season . . .
>
> Psalm 1:3

Fruit is proof of our identity

A few years back, my husband accepted a new position that resulted in us moving from Kentucky to Florida. When we moved into our new house, we realized that the previous owners left a ton of great stuff behind: two porch sets, various garden goodies, and lots of plants in really nice pottery. My guess is that since they were moving from Florida to North Carolina, they figured their tropicals wouldn't be happy in the mountains. Whether they just ran out of time to try to sell the plants or intentionally wanted them to go to us, I am grateful! I love all the green it brings to our back porch. The first month we lived there was consumed with unpacking and settling in, so I didn't get to checking on the plants for several weeks.

The tree in the farthest corner of our porch looked a bit different from the rest, so I went back to check on it. Turns out, it was a fake Ficus tree! I have no idea why it was set in the corner of the porch, exposed to direct sun and rainfall, but this seven-foot silk plant was ruined. The basket it sat in was soggy and breaking apart, and the leaves were beginning to turn a bluish shade, thanks to the bleaching of the sun. Through all the craziness of moving in, we never noticed that this fake tree was sitting out among the living ones. Yet over time it became obvious that this tree was not real. Just because it was in the right place—where you would expect a tree to be—and even though it was surrounded by trees that were thriving, that didn't make it a real tree.

Beyond the porch, in our backyard, we have four citrus trees. After a year of living here, some of the trees began to bear fruit. What we thought were identical plantings were actually different varieties. One proved to be a lemon tree, another a grapefruit, and yet another an orange tree. There is one that has yet to bear fruit, so we are still not sure exactly what type of citrus tree it is. The fruit each tree put out gave us proof of its identity. A cactus will never bear grapes. A gardenia bush will never put out roses. A lemon tree will never produce pineapples. So it is with the Happy Soul. We are known and identified by our Happy fruit. A sick and sinful soul will never produce Happy Soul fruit. Being in the right places, among the right people, is not enough to make us a Happy Soul.

The term *Christian* (just like the word *happiness*) can be used in different ways by different people. I mentioned before that I grew up thinking that because I was in Christian places, among Christian people, that I must also be a Christian. I've had many conversations with people who, when asked when they became a Christian, answer that they've always been a Christian. You and I discussed early on that we become a Christian only by the grace of God, through our faith in the sacrifice of Jesus. Yet some among us are actually fake Ficus.

On the other end of the spectrum are those who are truly saved but are uncertain if it "took." I spent many years worrying if I was truly saved. Did I say the prayer right? Did I give enough of my heart to God? How can I be *sure* that I am going to spend eternity with God?

If you, like me, have ever wondered if your salvation is real, we need to understand that true faith always produces true fruit. It is what Happy Souls do. They show happy fruit. A true Happy planting of the Lord will always exhibit evidence of its inner identity through the bearing of the fruit of the Spirit. Once I truly saw my need for Jesus—because I could never be good enough to make it to God on my own—I began to grow. Fruit began to show. My internal identity became an external reality. I now bear the undeniable fruit of a Happy Soul.

A good tree doesn't produce bad fruit; on the other hand, a bad tree doesn't produce good fruit. For each tree is known by its own fruit. Figs aren't gathered from thornbushes, or grapes picked from a bramble bush.

Luke 6:43–44

Fruit is proof of His presence

And I pray this: that your love will keep on growing in knowledge and every kind of discernment, so that you may approve the things that are superior and may be pure and blameless in the day of Christ, filled with the fruit of righteousness that comes through Jesus Christ to the glory and praise of God.

Philippians 1:9–11

Not only did previous owners leave behind pots and plants, they also added features to the home and yard we probably never would have spent the time or money on, yet we are enjoying them tremendously. For example, the original owners had a well dug when the house was built. The owners after them had the property professionally landscaped with beautiful plants and decorative pavers. To keep it thriving, they also installed an extensive sprinkler system with several zones and drip irrigation hoses. We rarely have to think about keeping the yard green. The best thing about it all is that the whole watering system is drawn from the well, which means we don't have to pay for all that water! We can allow the system to run on schedule without fear of a huge water bill. Our beautiful, fruitful, happy backyard is evidence of the careful planning of the previous owners and the life-sustaining presence of the abundant (free!) well water.

The fruitful, beautiful state of our backyard is due to it being well-watered. The Happy Soul will also be fruitful as a result of being well-watered. Fruit is the undeniable proof of being unshakably planted in the presence of God. Where there are deep roots, there will always be fruitfulness.

Old Katie likes to get stuff done. Old Katie doesn't like people. People get in her way and mess up her stuff. Old Katie just wants to be left alone to get her stuff done and to reach her goals. Old Katie = Bulldozer Katie. Get in her way and you better watch out. Bulldozer Katie still tries to show her ugly head. But God has done a great work in me, and Bulldozer Katie is no longer who I am. I am Happy Katie. And I now know—without a shadow of a doubt—that God has done and is doing a great work in me. I can say this with confidence because I can see fruit. There is outward evidence of my Happy Soul reality. I now have the ability to be patient. I can put the needs and desires of others before my own. I can hold my tongue and not lash out when someone gets in my way. I can forgive and forgive (and forgive again) because of the life-giving presence of Jesus in my life. This doesn't mean I choose patience and selflessness and self-control every time. I don't. (Remember, there is an internal battle between our old self and our new.) But there are times where I can step back and clearly see the fruit of God's Spirit in my life. Especially in light of my old bulldozer self who used to run rampant within me, any sort of selfless care shown to others by me is the fruit of Jesus in me. Period.

If you are a follower of Christ, there ought to be much in your life that you can point to as the fruit of His presence, something that is clearly the evidence of a work of God in you. To the Happy Soul, over time, there are certain sins that used to entangle her that are no longer palatable. The Happy Soul has a greater and growing obedience to God's Way. Her interactions with others are marked by God's presence. His character becomes her character. The Happy Soul is fruitful: love, joy, peace, patience, kindness, goodness, faithfulness, gentleness, self-control are what she is known for (Galatians 5:22–23). But this fruit cannot and will not come without a deep planting into the soil of God's character. The Happy, fruitful Soul is dependent on God's provision.

> Remain in me, and I in you. Just as a branch is unable to produce fruit by itself unless it remains on the vine, neither can you unless you remain in me. I am the vine; you are the branches. The one who remains in me and I in him produces much fruit, because you can do nothing without me.
>
> John 15:4–5

> My Father is glorified by this: that you produce much fruit and prove to be my disciples.
>
> John 15:8

The Happy Soul Is Resilient

> He is like a tree planted beside flowing streams . . .
> and whose leaf does not wither.
>
> Psalm 1:3

Not only is the Happy Soul fruitful, it is resilient. The fact that we need resiliency, though, points to the reality of the broken world we live in. It's not a matter of *if* we walk through the fire. It's a matter of *when*. Each of us will walk through our own hard times and heartbreak. We all experience suffering and sorrow. But the Happy Soul is resilient—whatever comes her way.

Several years ago, a moment came I never imagined I would face when I lost my younger brother to a drug overdose. I found myself at the funeral home, signing the papers of my brother's death certificate, after which I walked into the adjacent room to say good-bye to James. That cold November day in the wood-paneled viewing room was the last time all six of us were together.

Of course, James was already gone, but his twenty-nine-year-old body lay in front of us in a stark pine box, ready for cremation. My parents, myself, and my two remaining siblings, Nathan and Sarah, all stood in a line parallel to the box. We were frozen together, about four feet off from the casket, not quite sure what to do, what to say, or how to say good-bye. I can't remember who went first, but one by one we each traveled those long, painful forty-eight inches to say good-bye.

My turn came and, as I walked toward James, my eyes played tricks on me. His chest seemed to raise and lower. Part of me expected him to pop up out of that box *Candid Camera*–style and join the family gathering. But he couldn't be moving. It wasn't possible. He had been dead for days. My eyes envisioned what my heart longed for. Breath. Life. A second chance.

He never did sit up. I placed my hand on his cold cheek, kissed his forehead, and said good-bye. The memory of these moments brings a grief just as fresh as it first arrived the moment I received the news. I am unable to write this story without weeping.

Grief is a peculiar yet inescapable emotion—and it's a given in this fallen world. This desolation of the soul wears many badges. We often think of grief as a natural, gut-wrenching response to death, but it doesn't stop there. There are many and varied types of losses that can usher in the same paralysis and pain as a loss of life does. It might be the relationship, child, or dream that never came to be; the slow erosion of a friendship, career, or a marriage; the debilitating depression, physical weakness, or lonely infertility. Grief is ubiquitous to life in this sin-stained world.

Those first few weeks of walking through the news of James's death, I was filled with confusion, especially since his death was unexpected and premature. My gut reaction to grief was questions.

What just happened?

Why did this happen?

Where was God through all of this?

Why didn't He stop it from happening?

How do I move on from here?

Why does it have to be this way?

Honestly, now that I've been assaulted by grief, it oftentimes leaves me afraid. The loss of my brother was hard. But I've yet to lose a child, a husband, or a parent. My deepest fears have not been realized. Oftentimes, when a family member calls me at an atypical time, a part of me freezes up. I answer the phone—holding my breath—bracing for bad news. My mind all-too-easily wanders toward all sorts of scenarios involving fires, accidents, or abductions. The thought of losing anyone else is paralyzing. But I know more loss is bound to come. I am not promised tomorrow with anyone. So yet other questions I find myself asking are

What's next?

Will He ask me to walk through the death of a child? The premature death of my husband?

What heartbreak is around the corner?

> Lord, listen to my voice;
> let your ears be attentive to my cry for help.
>
> Psalm 130:2

Stockpile truth

Growing up in California, we were taught what to do in case of earthquakes. Once I moved to Alabama, I had to learn what to do during the threat of a tornado. When we lived in Kentucky, we had to prepare for severe snowstorms. In Florida, it is hurricanes we hunker down for. With each of these threats, there are safeguards taken and supplies gathered. The goal is to be ready for the worst-case scenario. Whether it be bread and milk, gas and water, batteries and canned goods, firewood and extra blankets, each possibility for a natural disaster demands its own stockpiles. Just as it would be foolish to fail to prepare for a impending hurricane, we must not be fools when it comes to grief. The Happy Soul expects and prepares for it. The Happy Soul gears up for grief.

The unexpected loss of James knocked the wind out of me for a while. But it didn't take me down. I never once doubted the good character of God. It's not that I understood His timing. It's not that I didn't ask why James had to struggle the way he did. It's that I was driven more by what I knew to be true about God—that He is an all-knowing, all-loving, in-control God. But without this foundation—twenty years of studying God's Word and stockpiling truth—my experience of James's death most definitely would have been different.

The biblical truth we gather up when our soul is thriving is the nourishment our hearts will feed off of when we're barely hanging on. This is a mark of the Happy Soul. Resiliency, no matter what comes her way. When the waves of grief pound her hard, it will be the firm and steadfast grip she *already* has on truth that will keep her from being tossed, tattered, and torn when tragedy strikes. This doesn't mean she won't question or weep or writhe in pain. But it does mean that—regardless of her circumstances—she will experience a peace that surpasses understanding, a joy indescribable, and a spiritual nearness to God even when every cell within her screams, "My God, my God. Why have you abandoned me?" When we have truth stored up within us, we can preach those truths to our hearts during the darkest of hours. Holding on to the truth He's given us is how we keep our leaves from withering.

Our questions and doubts do not scare or offend God. He knows and understands our frailty and fallenness way more than we do. We don't need to hide our questions from God, but we do need to recognize the bigger picture: the fact that we see in a mirror dimly and have limited knowledge of God and His beautiful ways (1 Corinthians 13:12). God is powerfully, perennially, and perfectly doing a million good works, of which our pain and sorrow are all encompassed. From this earthly view, we will never come close to beholding or understanding the marvelous, intricate, and one day perfectly complete work of God. We must hold a firm grip on the good character of God and His ability to work all our painful experiences together for His glory (Romans 8:28).

This is the resiliency we receive when our life is founded on who God is. Instead of being tossed around and victimized by the waves, we can hold on to hope through the storms. He never promises us that the storms will cease. He promises to hold us through the squall. The Happy Soul is not exempt from trouble, but the Happy Soul has the comfort of God to guide her through it. But we have to stay saturated by the Source in order to benefit from this strength. The Happy, resilient Soul is dependent on God's provision.

> My God, my God, why have you abandoned me?
> Why are you so far away when I groan for help?
> Every day I call to you, my God, but you do not answer.
> Every night I lift my voice, but I find no relief.
> Yet you are holy,
> enthroned on the praises of Israel.
> Our ancestors trusted in you,
> and you rescued them.

They cried out to you and were saved.
They trusted in you and were never disgraced.

Psalm 22:1–5 NLT

Use Up the Stockpile

We often think of the book of Psalms as a happy book filled with praise and worship. Yet over a third of the Psalms are filled with lament. They question. They complain. They cry out. However, alongside the wails, there is worship—a declaration of God's good and steadfast character. They exhibit a deep trust in His faithful love and unchanging righteousness. The sad and sullen psalmists stood steady with an unwavering trust in the truth of who God is. Twice in Psalm 42 and once in chapter 43, we see the same set of phrases addressing the soul: "Why are you cast down, O my soul, and why are you in turmoil within me? Hope in God; for I shall again praise him, my salvation and my God." The psalmist told his soul what to do and feel. So also must the Happy Soul.

The Happy Soul wrestles with her hard reality, then instructs her heart what to do while she waits for God's rescue.

The Happy Soul presents her doubts and questions to God, then sermonizes her soul toward the truth of His character.

The Happy Soul laments all she's lost, but she also prompts her spirit toward the ever-present hope she has through Christ.

This life is hard. It's okay to waver. To question. To grieve. To be conflicted. However, as we do, we must cling to truth. But if we are going to cling to truth through our troubles, we need a solid foundation of who God is. Do you see how each secret builds on one another? Focus leads to resolve. Resolve leads to attachment. Attachment leads to dependency. Dependency leads to a fruitful resiliency that will carry us through the storm.

We cannot tell ourselves what is true of God if we aren't sure of Him to begin with. God sees. God cares. God heals. God controls. God comforts. God loves. God is good. Do you believe it? Do you know it deep down in your soul? Do you know where in Scripture it tells you these things? It will be these truths—and the conviction of their validity—that will allow you to walk with hope in God amidst the everyday hardships and the unthinkable tragedies. Instead of being driven by our ever-changing emotions, let's embed our anchor firmly in the bedrock of God's unchanging character and steadfast love.

> The person who trusts in the LORD,
> whose confidence indeed is the LORD, is blessed.
> He will be like a tree planted by water:
> it sends its roots out toward a stream,
> it doesn't fear when heat comes,
> and its foliage remains green.
> It will not worry in a year of drought
> or cease producing fruit.
>
> Jeremiah 17:7–8

This beautiful parallel passage in Jeremiah is very similar to our Psalm 1 passage. But it provides us with a few extra details about the Happy Soul. The Happy Soul *does not fear* the fires around the corner. The Happy Soul *does not worry* during her desperate times of drought. Why? Because she is planted by the streams of God and has solidly situated herself in the banks of His character. She will be evergreen and resiliently fruitful—no matter what comes her way. Her source of support is in the stream. The enduring fruit of God's people stems from the sustaining power of God.

James's death was hard. The reality of his death *is still hard*. I'm certain that around the corner lies harder things still. But through all the ups and downs, through all the pain and problems, I can be a Happy Soul—not because I am strong and steady but because my God is. You can be a Happy Soul too! We don't have to fear the future. We can kick anxiety good-bye. We can thrive regardless of our circumstances. We can never cease to bear fruit. This is the reality of the Happy Soul who trusts in the Lord. She knows that He is a good and powerful, personal and great God who will provide for her every step of whatever comes her way. The Happy Soul is dependent on God's provision.

> Consider it a great joy, my brothers and sisters, whenever you experience various trials, because you know that the testing of your faith produces endurance. And let endurance have its full effect, so that you may be mature and complete, lacking nothing.
>
> James 1:2–4

11

Develop Deep Roots

I am God Almighty.
Live in my presence and be blameless.

Genesis 17:1

Not too long ago I found myself in another dark place. After four years of church ministry in Kentucky, it had become clear that God was asking us to begin searching for our next assignment. Over those four years, there were times when I was ready to give up and move on. But my husband, Chris, wasn't. Then there were times when I was hopeful and excited and ready to conquer all the mountains, while Chris was uncertain he was the one who could lead the church into the future. We rode that teeter-totter back and forth for years.

At this point, a bit more than four years in, it had been the longest we'd lived anywhere in our fourteen years of marriage. Our kids were seven, five, and three when we moved to Kentucky. In many ways, our life in Kentucky was most of what they remembered. The last thing I wanted to do was uproot our family again. But through many different signals, including the fact that both Chris and I were on the same page—ready and willing to move on, if that's what God wanted—it was becoming more and more clear that it was time to leave.

Though it would be over a year before we moved, I almost immediately began mourning the loss. We had made dear friends, but suddenly there was this huge change looming and I couldn't talk to any of them about it. I couldn't tell them Chris was looking for another job. I couldn't tell them their pastor was leaving them. I couldn't tell them how excited I was for what God had next for us. I couldn't tell them how sad I was to say good-bye. I couldn't tell them that I felt more isolated than I've ever felt. I was surrounded by people I loved and trusted, yet a huge part of my heart was unknown by them.

Walking through those really difficult weeks, I was forced to make a choice: to believe all I knew to be true about God and His Word, or wallow in all the what-ifs and why-nots. I certainly had moments of wallowing and worrying, but ultimately I chose His presence. I remained in the Word, even when it was hard to get out of bed. I asked Him for help. He provided a friend outside of the church for me to talk to. He gave me the courage to talk to my doctor about medication. Without the promises of His Word and the guiding of His presence, that time could have consumed me. There were definitely days where it did, but overall, my root system kept me well-watered.

How to Develop a Deep Root System

Becoming deeply grounded involves a multi-layered effort to know, love, and depend on God and all He's given us. The Bible is filled with truths and promises that inform us toward how to stay plugged in to those benefits. There are three main actions that will assist us in our efforts to remain connected to God's presence.

Keep your confidence in the capability of the Father.

Keep your steps in sync with the Spirit.

Keep your eyes on the example of Christ.

Keep your confidence in the capability of the Father

Look, I am the Lord, the God over every creature. Is anything too difficult for me?

Jeremiah 32:27

If we say we believe in God and in the promises of His Word, then every hard season, every temptation to sin, every doubt that darkens our door is an opportunity for us to act on what we say we believe. Are we going to be driven by our fears and feelings? Or are we going to be tethered by the truth about our Savior: that He is mighty to save (Zephaniah 3:17)? Peter tells us that God's "divine power has given us everything required for life and godliness" (2 Peter 1:3). Paul says that our "God is able to make every grace overflow to you, so that in every way, always having everything you need, you may excel in every good work" (2 Corinthians 9:8). The successful Christian life is ours in Christ! The Happy Soul life is available every moment. In order to experience it, we must act on what we believe and stand firm on God's faithfulness.

Jesus once said, "With man this is impossible, but with God all things are possible" (Matthew 19:26). This statement is often taken out of context. Here he was talking with His disciples about how hard it is to enter the Kingdom of God. The disciples, thinking it impossible for anyone to meet the salvation requirements, asked Jesus, "Then who can be saved?" He answered this question with the truth that all things are possible with God. Another often-misused verse is Philippians 4:13: "I am able to do all things through him who strengthens me." The context here is one of contentment. Paul states that he's seen it all. He's been well fed and gone hungry. He's lived in seasons of great abundance and through periods of severe need. And through it all, God has sustained him; therefore, whatever else is around the corner, Paul knows that he can walk through anything by the strength of Christ.

So many view these verses like they are an energy shot we take before a run. But you and I will never become strong enough to climb every mountain and slay every giant. The common denominator between these two verses is that we are utterly unable, but God is altogether able. He is able to bring us from spiritual death to life. He is able to change our hearts. He is able to give us exactly what we need to get through whatever comes our way. But the strength of God is not what we ought to seek. The strength we receive is a by-product of being with Him.

When I am depressed and lonely, I can have strength to sail through the storm, as I remember that I am actually never alone. He will never leave me or forsake me (Hebrews 13:5–6).

When I am exhausted and discouraged and want to give up, I can have endurance to keep going, as I remember that God is always working even when I cannot see it (Philippians 1:6).

When I have sinned and stumbled and experience the crippling feelings of failure, I can rest in the reality that there is no condemnation for the child of God (Romans 8:1).

For every unhappy situation that comes our way, we can face it with great confidence that God will carry us through. God is "able to do above and beyond all that we ask or think according to the power that works in us" (Ephesians 3:20). He is "able to protect you from stumbling and to make you stand in the presence of his glory, without blemish and with great joy" (Jude 24). There is no situation that God will allow in your life that God's provision can't handle. But if we're not well-established, we will shrivel up at the first flicker of a flame. When hurricane seasons come, the trees with a healthy root base survive. The dead and dying are overturned.

Keep your steps in sync with the Spirit

If we live by the Spirit, let us also keep in step with the Spirit.

Galatians 5:25

Let's go back to the Old Testament covenant once again. God entered into the culture of ancient mankind and made an agreement with them to protect and provide for those who would follow His holy Way. God—holy and magnificent—came down to earth to dwell with His people. He manifested himself primarily through the typical mode of honoring deity at the time: temple worship. From temple-building instructions to daily temple practices, big chunks of the Old Testament are filled with directives and data on how to worship God. These commands were given to give His people a new and different way to worship, and the obedience to these commands preserved His presence within their midst, specifically in the temple. But even then, His presence in the temple was limited to certain spaces and particular people on behalf of the nation as a whole.

But then Jesus came and changed everything. He perfectly fulfilled the covenant law and became the once and final sacrifice needed to erase the guilt of our sin. And now the presence of God resides in a new home: the hearts of His people. "Don't you yourselves know that you are God's temple and that the Spirit of God lives in you?" (1 Corinthians 3:16). God still resides in the temple, but it is no longer a single stationary building. The dwelling place of God is within each Happy Soul. The holy offerings of God's people are no longer that of unblemished bulls and rams. They are now the holy and obedient lives of God's people. "Therefore, brothers and sisters, in view of the mercies of God, I urge you to present your bodies as a living sacrifice, holy and pleasing to God; this is your true worship" (Romans 12:1).

The Spirit of God has come to permanently dwell within us (Romans 8:9; Titus 3:6–7). He is the guarantee of all we can look forward to in eternity (Ephesians 1:13–14; 2 Corinthians 5:5). He gives us renewal and life (John 6:63; Titus 3:5). He enables us for the carrying out of God's plan (Acts 2:4; 1 Corinthians 12:7–11). God lives within us! And with His presence comes the ability to live the Happy Soul life.

A life of obedience is not reserved for the (fictitious) superhero breed of Christians. Every Christian can walk in obedience because every Christian has the Spirit of God within them. Unfortunately, so many believers miss the importance of this crucial truth. We get that we cannot save ourselves. We accept the sacrifice of Christ on the cross as our only way to spend eternity with God. However, we don't see that we also need God's help for obedience. The power of the gospel, which is present within us through the presence of God's Spirit, is not simply for our eternal security. This empowering fuel is also for our daily sanctification—our becoming more and more like Jesus.

> Are you so foolish? After beginning by the Spirit, are you now finishing by the flesh?
>
> Galatians 3:3

I say then, walk by the Spirit and you will certainly not carry out the desire of the flesh.

Galatians 5:16

The Spirit of God is within us and He is always moving, always working. But instead of joining in this work, we ignore it. Sometimes we stifle it. Instead of the presence of God permeating every part of our being, we've pushed Him down into the places where He can't be publicly seen.

For the entire fullness of God's nature dwells bodily in Christ, and you have been filled by him, who is the head over every ruler and authority.

Colossians 2:9–10

Though I was born and raised in Southern California, I've lived my entire adult life in the South, namely Florida, Georgia, Kentucky, and Alabama. I've become accustomed to Southern ways, but there are two things that I don't know if I will ever adopt: saying "y'all" and drinking sweet tea. Sweet tea is a big deal in the South; many Southerners don't realize that if they head north or travel west, their beloved drink disappears from restaurants. Many Southerners have found themselves out of sweet-tea country and have to settle for unsweetened tea. Then they attempt to make sweet tea by adding a few packets of sugar. Much to their dismay, this approach doesn't work. The sugar only settles to the bottom. The tea does not taste sweet.

I've never made sweet tea before, but I've seen both my husband and mother-in-law make it. According to them, a successful batch of sweet tea starts with the sugar already in the pitcher. Once the tea is brewed, the still-hot liquid is poured into the pitcher of sugar and the two become one. It is no longer sugar and hot tea in a pitcher. It is now the sought-after sweet tea, ready to be chilled and poured.

Many Christians live life thinking they can just add a dash of God to their day to make it sweet. We're like those poor sweet-tea Southerners who've wandered outside of the sweet-tea territory and think we can create that delightful drink on our own. We try a few "Christian" things as an attempt to fix the problem, when what we really need is to back up and allow the contents of our pitcher to be united with Christ. We need to be steeped in a continual communion with Him, because we can never be truly sweet on our own. We need the presence of God to permeate every part of us.

As we allow Him to fill our every moment, we are rewarded with renewal. Jesus promised as much: "If anyone is thirsty, let him come to me, and drink. The one who believes in me, as the Scripture has said, will have streams of living water flow from deep within him" (John 7:37–38). Here we see the same life-giving, satisfying streams we did in Psalm 1. This is not a superficial trickle. This is a deep, abundant source of life that comes from God that we ought to draw up from and allow to penetrate every part of our life.

> So then, just as you have received Christ Jesus as Lord, continue to live in him, being rooted and built up in him and established in the faith.
>
> Colossians 2:6–7

Keep your eyes on the example of Christ

Keeping our eyes on Jesus, the source and perfecter of our faith.

Hebrews 12:2

At least once a year we get together with my side of the family—typically during the week of Thanksgiving. We all descend on my parents' house, where my kids and their cousins (nine in all) blissfully greet one another, then promptly scatter throughout the house to play. Sometimes we have an outing or two planned, but often we just stay home. We don't have to have a bunch of activities to do; we simply dwell together as a family, enjoying each other's company.

The funny thing is, my sister and her family live about five minutes away from my parents. They could stay at home, in their own beds, with their own showers, and be much more comfortable than staying at my parents' house with eight adults and nine kids sharing two and a half bathrooms. But every year, they pack their suitcases for the week and plug in to the family fun. They do this because they want to be with the family. We all enjoy being together. We look forward to it all year. We crave time with one another and want to get every moment together we can. Likewise, staying plugged in to His presence is a lot like any other personal connection we value. It requires time and investment, communication and a continual commitment. Like Paul, who stated, "my goal is to know him" (Philippians 3:10) and "I also consider everything to be a loss in view of the surpassing value of knowing Christ Jesus my Lord" (Philippians 3:8), we need to make it our aim to keep our focus on knowing and loving Jesus better and better.

Planting ourselves into God's presence—making our home with Him—ought to be with the same determination and joy my sister and I do each fall vacation. The more we are with Jesus, the more we will look like Jesus.

> Jesus answered, "If anyone loves me, he will keep my word. My Father will love him, and we will come to him and make our home with him."
>
> John 14:23

I'm currently struggling with a particularly difficult person. I've been deeply wounded by their actions. It is a daily choice to not act on all the negative emotions I have toward her. In the past I ran headlong into sin when it came to difficult people, justifying my outburst of anger and putting them in their place with the fact that God has given me a high value on justice and truth-telling. I have trampled many people down under the guise of speaking the truth. The temptation is strong to do the same in this situation. But doing so would be forgetting Christ. I cannot be at home with Jesus and be at war with His people. And when I am truly at home with Christ, and keeping my eyes on who He is, it softens me. My hatred melts away. I remember that I have been a recipient of mercy, and that I am called to "adopt the same attitude as that of Christ Jesus" (Philippians 2:5).

> For I have given you an example, that you also should do just as I have done for you.
>
> John 13:15

Every encounter with a difficult person is a choice to act on what I say I believe: that God's Way is best. "Therefore, as God's chosen ones, holy and dearly loved, put on compassion, kindness, humility, gentleness, and patience, bearing with one another and forgiving one another if anyone has a grievance against another. Just as the Lord has forgiven you, so you are also to forgive" (Colossians 3:12–13). And though I don't *feel* like giving this person forgiveness and grace, I *know* that it is God's Way. Through His strength, His grace, and His guiding, I can love this person. We don't have to be best friends, I don't have to like her, but I don't need to hold on to hatred either.

Whatever you are going through, look to Jesus. Whatever difficult relationships you are walking through, whether it is a betrayal, a wounding, or another type of hurt, look to Jesus. Whatever situation has you tied-in-knots anxious or severely afraid of the future, look to Jesus. He has borne the pain inflicted by others. He has experienced incredibly stressful situations. He has been betrayed and ignored, forgotten and forsaken. He knows your pain. Through both His perfect example and powerful enabling to follow in His footsteps, He is the help you need.

> For we do not have a high priest who is unable to sympathize with our weaknesses, but one who has been tempted in every way as we are, yet without sin. Therefore, let us approach the throne of grace with boldness, so that we may receive mercy and find grace to help us in time of need.
>
> Hebrews 4:15–16

Practicalities for Building a Deep Root System

There are loads of ways to stay rooted in God's presence so actions will vary from person to person and season to season. To get you started, here is a list of brainstorms for building those roots.

- Write out a letter to God. Share your heart with Him. Confess your sins. Thank Him for who He is and all He's done for you. Ask Him for help with what you are struggling with.
- Find a worship playlist or grab an album that helps you remember the goodness of God.
- Study your Bible.
- Share what you are learning with Christian family and friends.

- Keep a gratitude journal where each day you recognize gifts that you are thankful for.
- Go to church and listen intently to the sermon. Take notes. Ask God what He wants you to do as a result of hearing the teaching.
- Memorize a passage of Scripture.
- Talk to God in the shower or on your morning commute.
- Read a book that points you to Jesus.
- Whisper your requests of help throughout your day.

These are all examples of staying plugged in to His presence. God is already with you. You don't have to go on a scavenger hunt to find Him. You simply need to take intentional steps to recognize Him in your day. Invite Him to fill every part of your life. Instead of throwing all our efforts toward a relegated "quiet time," let's make connecting with Him part of the very rhythm of our day. Yes, that will probably include still moments with your Bible open, ready to hear from God. But that is just the starting place—not the finish line—of connecting with God every day.

> I have asked one thing from the LORD;
> it is what I desire:
> to dwell in the house of the LORD
> all the days of my life,
> gazing on the beauty of the LORD
> and seeking him in his temple.
>
> Psalm 27:4

SOUL SEARCHING

Happy Soul Evaluation

How much fruit-filled confirmation is there in my life that I am a Happy Soul?

1........2........3........4........5........6........7........8........9........10
No external evidence   *Obvious and undeniable*

How resilient am I?

1........2........3........4........5........6........7........8........9........10
I melt at the first flicker of a flame   *Troubles throw me to God*

How active am I in pursuing the following?

Keeping my confidence in the capability of the Father.

1........2........3........4........5........6........7........8........9........10
No effort   *Excellent effort*

Keeping my steps in sync with the Spirit.

1........2........3........4........5........6........7........8........9........10
No effort   *Excellent effort*

Keeping my eyes on the example of Christ.

1........2........3........4........5........6........7........8........9........10
No effort   *Excellent effort*

Happy Soul Actions

Think through the situation that is most trying for you right now. What do you need from God that only He can give? Spend some time searching the Scriptures for truths that you need to cling to about who God is. There are many online Bible concordances that can help you find what you need. Also consider reaching out to a friend or mentor for help.

- Crippled by anxiety? Search for truths about God's faithfulness, peace, and care for His people.
- Consumed by grief? Search for truths about God's comforting presence.
- Crushed by guilt? Search for truths about God's mercy, forgiveness, and grace.

Jot down the truths you find.

Choose at least one action you will do today to be more rooted in the presence of God. Write it down below and ask God for the grace and strength to follow through.

Happy Soul Prayer

God, I am grateful that you have not left me to live this life on my own. You have given me everything I need to live a godly life, and though I don't always know or remember how to access those gifts of grace, you are still working in me. I thank you for the example of Christ recorded in your Word. Thank you for the presence of your Spirit within me. Thank you for the power I have through being with you. Thank you for your unending love and mercy toward me. I want to be deeply rooted in your presence. I don't want to live this life on my own. I long to live a successful Christian life—one that honors you and displays who you are to those around me. I cannot do this on my own. I need you.

SECRET #5

THE HAPPY SOUL
IS CONFIDENT
IN WHO SHE IS

12

Confident

For the LORD knows the way of the righteous,
but the way of the wicked will perish.

Psalm 1:6 ESV

My career as a med tech didn't last long. I worked in the hospital full time for six months before I joined the staff of Campus Crusade for Christ (now Cru) to work as a campus minister. My first eight months or so of my time with Cru were spent in training and raising support. Every penny I needed to live off of had to be found through the support of churches and individuals. So day after day, week after week, month after month, I made phone calls, met with people, and walked by faith that the finances I needed to make it to campus would arrive.

Raising full-time support was one of the hardest things I've had to do—especially up to that point in my twentysomething life. It was emotionally draining and disappointing. I was treated poorly by some people. I was avoided and ignored. One response in particular came through a return letter. It was truly kind and respectful, but straightforward in the fact that they could not offer financial support and that it would be better off for society if I continued in my chosen profession of medical technology. *For real, those words were in the letter.* In their defense, they had walked away from belief in the God they grew up with. (Looking back, it was probably silly of me to send a letter.) It was this person's belief that God is the result of hallucinations and overactive imaginations of a less-civilized and mentally under-developed ancient people. So this assessment of my pursuits makes sense: If God doesn't exist, then why should a young graduate waste her education to go tell college students about Jesus?

Though initially discouraging, this letter was merely a bump in the road. Their lostness lay heavy on my heart (still does), but it didn't throw me off my track. It didn't shake my confidence. I knew—without a doubt—that the God of the Bible exists. I knew what He had called me to. And I knew that He would provide all I needed. There is great strength found in knowing who we are, what our calling is, and that the One who calls us holds unlimited resources. When we know who God says we are, the words of others don't hold as much power over us.

The Happy Soul Knows Who She Is Because of Jesus

Dear friends, we are God's children now.

1 John 3:2

Thanks to the Netflix show *The Crown*, I've learned much about Queen Elizabeth II of England. But even though you could say that I now know a lot *about* her Majesty, I certainly do not *know* her personally. Knowing about and actually knowing are two very different things. Do you remember back when we talked about Jesus being the Door of the sheep—the only way to God? In that same passage, Jesus tells us that "I am the good shepherd. I know my own and my own know me" (John 10:14). Here we see that Jesus' sheep are His "own," and it is His sheep—and His sheep alone— that He *knows* in this special way.

This special type of knowing is made even more clear in Matthew 7:15–23 when Jesus said, "Not everyone who says to me, 'Lord, Lord,' will enter the kingdom of heaven, but the one who does the will of my Father who is in heaven. On that day many will say to me, 'Lord, Lord, did we not prophesy in your name, and cast out demons in your name, and do many mighty works in your name?' And then will I declare to them, 'I never knew you; depart from me, you workers of lawlessness.'" Did God *know about* those who called Him "Lord, Lord"? Yes, He knew about them. He created them. He knows every hair on their head. He knows when they sleep and when they rise. But the knowing Jesus refers to in Matthew 7:23 and John 10:14 is a different type of knowing. It is an eternal intimacy. A status of salvation from sins. It is a *knowing* that stems from the surrender of a soul who has entered into a relationship with God through the sacrifice of Jesus. God *knows* the Happy Soul. The Happy Soul is a recipient of mercy and a beneficiary of grace.

> Nevertheless, God's solid foundation stands firm, bearing this inscription: The Lord knows those who are his.
>
> 2 Timothy 2:19a

Recipient of mercy

> The one enthroned in heaven
> . . . speaks to them in his anger
> and terrifies them in his wrath.
>
> Psalm 2:4–5

> Blessed is the one whose transgression is forgiven,
> whose sin is covered.
> Blessed is the man against whom the LORD counts no
>   iniquity,
> and in whose spirit there is no deceit.
>
> Psalm 32:1–2 ESV

The wrath of God is not typically a popular topic of discussion. For me, I was tempted to leave these truths out of our discussion altogether. There is a desire within me to downplay these words, but this is our reality: God is a holy God of righteous judgment, and sinners cannot stand before Him. It is right for God to condemn any and every one of us to hell, because we deserve it. The wages of sin—what we earned because of our sin—is death (Romans 6:23). Both physical and spiritual. And it's not about how much sin we've done or not done, it's that we've sinned at all. Just once is enough to separate us from Him forever. Just one offense demands a death sentence. Every soul on this earth has earned the wrath of God. This is not a happy pill to swallow. But it is a truth the Happy Soul must have rooted deep within her. Because when we *really* get the punishment we deserve and *really* understand the mercy we've been given instead, it changes us.

I had an unfortunate event recently that perhaps you can relate to. We live near a lake, and the road that skirts the contours of the lake has a stunning view and a super-slow speed limit. A few weeks ago, I was driving home in a bit of a hurry, and as I turned into my neighborhood, a police officer was waiting for me. He'd already clocked me via his radar gun at 44 mph. The speed limit there is 30 mph. It's been decades since I have been pulled over and I was literally thirty seconds from home. Let me tell you, it was incredibly embarrassing to get pulled over in my own neighborhood for all to see. I was hoping to receive a small "slow down, ma'am" lecture instead of a ticket . . . but it didn't happen. However, he did show me some mercy. He officially recorded me at 36 mph in a 30 mph zone instead of the 44 mph he caught me doing. This resulted in a $131 fine instead of $206.

I was speeding. I deserved the ticket. It was 100 percent right for this man—who was hired to enforce the law—to pull me over and issue me a ticket for not following the law. And if I had been speeding in *your* neighborhood, near *your* children, grandchildren, or nieces and nephews you love, you would be demanding that I receive the punishment I deserve. It would have been right for him to write me up for a $206 ticket instead of a $131 one. But he showed me mercy. He withheld the full punishment and fine I deserved. So too has God withheld our deserved punishment.

> For you are not a God who delights in wickedness;
> evil cannot dwell with you.
> The boastful cannot stand in your sight;
> you hate all evildoers.
> You destroy those who tell lies;
> the LORD abhors violent and treacherous people.
>
> Psalm 5:4–6

> Therefore the wicked will not stand up in the judgment,
> nor sinners in the assembly of the righteous.
>
> Psalm 1:5

Some teach that this God of judgment and wrath is the God of the Old Testament, but not the God of the New Testament. They say that He's changed over time. He's grown. Some also say that since God's wrath seen clearly in the Old Testament has been satisfied through Christ, we no longer need to study or think about the wrath of God. It has no place in our discussions of the New

Testament God. I wholeheartedly disagree with these teachings. Scripture is not meant to be read with a Sharpie. Nor do we have the authority to disregard the lines we don't want to hear. All Scripture is inspired by God and profitable to us (2 Timothy 3:16). All of it. And the Bible is clear that God's wrath against sin burns just as bright as it always has.

> God is a righteous judge
> and a God who shows his wrath every day.
> Psalm 7:11

If someone were to walk into our church on a Sunday morning and yell out a death threat to my husband, Chris (he's the preacher), then run off, the cops would likely be called, a description of the incident and the perpetrator would be collected, and everyone would probably be on the alert for a while. But unless they caught the person in the act, no action could or would be taken.

However, say the same man cast the exact same threatening words toward the president of the United States of America. The threat would be contained immediately, an arrest made, and legal action taken. That same offense made to my husband, by the same perpetrator, would be handled with less seriousness than an offense against the U.S. president. Why? Because the gravity of the offense is directly tied to the position of the offended. A threat to my husband (though serious and scary) is not nearly as offensive in the eyes of the law as a threat to the office of the president. So it is—and infinitely more so—with God. The gravity of our sin problem is directly connected to the perfection and grandeur and power and holiness and sovereignty of our God.

God is completely without sin; therefore, our sin is categorically offensive to Him. And by offensive, I don't mean that He's just kinda annoyed by it, like a mosquito buzzing in His ear. Our sin is detestable to God. And because He is completely and infinitely righteous and holy, our sin is completely and infinitely offensive. Every act of sin is an act of rebellion.

> Why do the nations rage
> and the peoples plot in vain?
> The kings of the earth take their stand,
> and the rulers conspire together
> against the Lord and his Anointed One:
>
> Psalm 2:1–2

For all have sinned and fall short of the glory of God.

Romans 3:23

And you were dead in your trespasses and sins in which you previously lived according to the ways of this world, according to the ruler of the power of the air, the spirit now working in the disobedient. We too all previously lived among them in our fleshly desires, carrying out the inclinations of our flesh and thoughts, and we were by nature children under wrath as the others were also.

Ephesians 2:1–3

I was spiritually dead.

I lived according to the world.

I followed the ruler of the power of the air (Satan).

I was disobedient.

I followed the desires of my flesh.

I was inclined toward evil desires and thoughts.

I was under the wrath of God.

This is my ugly reality. It's yours too. Yet for the Happy Soul, this reality is a thing of the past. It is no longer who we are, because our story didn't end there. The good news is, the ones whom he *knows*—the Happy Souls—are indeed fortunate and free. The wrath of God toward them has been satisfied through the cross of Christ. But those who have yet to come to Christ—those whom He does not *know*—are still objects of God's wrath.

> But God, who is rich in mercy, because of his great love that he had for us, made us alive with Christ even though we were dead in trespasses.
>
> Ephesians 2:4–5

I don't have to look far to see the wickedness of my heart on full display. There is no denying my sin problem. I feel anything *but* righteous. But remember part of the foundational status we have as a Happy Soul? We are justified. Justification is the legal position that He declares over us when we trust in Christ as our only hope for eternity with God. Though I deserve to be condemned, when I put my faith in Christ's perfect obedience and His sufficient work on the cross to pay the penalty of my sins, my sin debt was paid for and a relationship with God was made possible. My problem was fixed. God's wrath toward my sin has been satisfied. (This is where we all proclaim, "Hallelujah!")

> And when you were dead in trespasses and in the uncircumcision of your flesh, he made you alive with him and forgave us all our trespasses. He erased the certificate of debt, with its obligations, that was against us and opposed to us, and has taken it away by nailing it to the cross.
>
> Colossians 2:13–14

So now, because I am *known* by God, I am no longer separated from Him because of my sin. I am justified before God. My status has changed from sinner to saint. In the highest, holy court, my case has been tried and I have been declared not guilty.

This is an incredible mercy.

I deserve the wrath of God. I am, without God, a wicked soul. But God rescued me. He has withheld His wrath from me and placed it on Christ.

I am a recipient of mercy. My only part was faith—faith in these facts: I am a sinner. Jesus is perfect. I deserve God's wrath. Jesus took that wrath for me. He is my only hope for an eternity with God. And this mercy now shapes everything I am and everything I do.

The Happy Soul is confident in who she is. She is a recipient of mercy.

> Once you were not a people, but now you are God's people; you had not received mercy, but now you have received mercy.
>
> 1 Peter 2:10

Beneficiary of grace

> For you, LORD, bless the righteous one;
> you surround him with favor like a shield.
>
> Psalm 5:12

> He has rescued us from the domain of darkness and transferred us into the kingdom of the Son he loves.
>
> Colossians 1:13

God did not stop at showing us mercy! Driven by His love for us, the punishment we deserved was withheld and redirected to Christ. This would have been enough to satisfy the perfection and judgment of God. We were brought out of the negative. But in the same moment that we were declared blameless, by the same love that drove His mercy, we were also given grace. Mercy and grace are different demonstrations of God's love for us.

Mercy is the withholding of a deserved punishment.

Grace is the bestowing of an undeserved present.

His mercy saved us from punishment, but that is only half the story. Not only did God take away my sins and put them on Christ, He took Christ's perfection and put it on me. The perfect One who never sinned took on my sin "so that in him we might become the righteousness of God" (2 Corinthians 5:21). His righteous life was credited to me, just as if I'd lived it myself! This triumphant exchange of my sin for Christ's perfection changes everything about me. So when God the Father sees me right now, in this very moment—though I yell at my kids and my heart is full of selfishness and my mind is filled with constant criticism—God sees the righteousness of Christ in me.

> The righteousness of God is through faith in Jesus Christ to all who believe.
>
> Romans 3:22

For every Happy Soul, this righteousness is our new inheritance, our new identity, and our new calling. We are new creatures (2 Corinthians 5:17). We have been born again to walk in newness of life (Romans 6:4). We now belong to the assembly of the righteous mentioned in Psalm 1. And the righteousness of Christ is just the beginning. The Bible—which itself is a gift of grace—is filled with evidences of God's abounding compassion toward us.

> Blessed is the God and Father of our Lord Jesus Christ, who has blessed us with every spiritual blessing in the heavens in Christ. For he chose us in him, before the foundation of the world, to be holy and blameless in love before him. He predestined us to be adopted as sons through Jesus Christ for himself, according to the good pleasure of his will, to the praise of his glorious grace that he lavished on us in the Beloved One. In him we have redemption through his blood, the forgiveness of our trespasses, according

to the riches of his grace that he richly poured out on us with all wisdom and understanding.

Ephesians 1:3–8

We are blessed with every spiritual blessing.

We have been chosen to be holy and blameless.

We have been adopted into the family of God.

We have redemption through Christ.

The riches of God's glorious grace have been lavished—richly poured out—on us through Christ.

We are recipients of mercy and heirs of grace. Out of this identity ought to spring up within us a well of worship.

He himself bore our sins in his body on the tree; so that, having died to sins, we might live for righteousness.

1 Peter 2:24

The Happy Soul Knows Why She Exists

And he died for all so that those who live should no longer live for themselves, but for the one who died for them and was raised.

2 Corinthians 5:15

My husband's first full-time pastoral position was in a small town in Florida. It is *literally* a one-stoplight town. There was no decent grocery store, no Starbucks, no Panera, no Target . . . not even a McDonald's or a Walmart. It is an agriculturally driven community, and a whole new world to this suburban-born girl. Chris was a youth pastor at the time and I vividly remember when we first met the kids in the youth group. Just about every one was wearing some sort of camo or cowboy boots, even the girls. I'd never realized there were so many different colors of camouflage!

Many of the kids were heavily involved in FFA (Future Farmers of America. I had no idea what it was and had to Google it when we first moved). They rode horses, grew watermelons, and raised pigs and chickens for show. It's kind of a big deal in those parts.

The first summer we lived there, everyone asked if we were going to visit the fair. Our kids were all under five at the time, and we thought the older two would enjoy going. I have fond childhood memories of the fair, filled with carnival games and petting zoos, Ferris wheels and funnel cakes. So we talked it up with the kids and we were all excited to go! We arrived on the scene and it was then that I realized that my suburban Southern California fair memories were a far cry from any memories my kids would have of the Levy County Fair.

There were no rides, and very few activities and food vendors. The heart of the fair attractions was in the main exhibition hall/ barn. What was drawing the community in wasn't the rides or concessions. It was the competitions. Though we didn't get to stay very long (see earlier family demographic detail of having three kids under five), we were able to watch a few of our youth show the pigs they'd fattened up, the watermelons they'd tended to, and the chickens they'd cared for from an embryonic state.

They were all very proud of their achievements—and rightly so! Some of them received ribbons, and they were proudly displayed on the animal cages and/or baskets of abundant produce. The fruit of their labors, their FFA glory—whether that was in plumage, foliage, or poundage—pointed the crowds to the hard work of their owners.

Similarly, we also exist to point others to our Owner. We were gifted life, specifically planted, and have been continually sustained by God for a purpose: We get to give our Blue Ribbon best and let the glory of the Gardener shine through us as we live out

His plan for our life. God has placed us around others who desperately need the salvation we've received, and as they interact with us, God's plan is for them to see our fruit—the evidence of the new life that is within us. God planted every believer in his or her particular time in history and place on the globe in order that they may be fruitful, so that all souls surrounding God's followers will see the holy-Happy evidence of His presence within them. All of this for one main goal: the glory of God.

Jesus himself confirmed this truth: "My Father is glorified by this: that you produce much fruit and prove to be my disciples" (John 15:8). Paul echoes the same idea about our purpose to glorify God with our lives in his letter to the church at Ephesus: "For he chose us in him, before the foundation of the world, to be holy and blameless in love before him" (Ephesians 1:4). We exist to be a fragrant aroma—a whiff of hope—to those who are perishing. And as we become known by the righteous and resilient fruit that is unexplainable—our love for the unlovable, our joy and peace during the unthinkable, our patience with the unbearable—the world takes notice and ultimately God is glorified.

It's easy to fall into the trap that the end goal of our life is to become a successful, productive member of society. Be the best version of you you can be, then sit back and enjoy the fruit of your labors. This is what most of us have been given as the prescription for happiness. But this is not a biblical picture of why we exist. We exist to glorify God. It is the reason we were rescued from sin, the reason we were given grace, the reason our heart still beats.

> All your people will be righteous;
> they will possess the land forever;
> they are the branch I planted,

the work of my hands,
so that I may be glorified.

Isaiah 60:21

I've been slowly working on our backyard. Though it is nice and green and beautifully paved, I'm not in love with the arrangement of plants. Whenever I get a few moments of free time in the early evening, once the Florida heat begins to lessen, you can find me digging up and replanting plants. Some of them are growing great but have outgrown their spot. Others are struggling because they are not getting enough sun. Some are getting too much. So I keep my hands busy in the garden, giving attention to each plant to find the perfect situation for each, but always keeping in mind the big-picture view.

With the same intentionality and care, each of us has been hand-placed by God exactly where we are. You and I are part of His big-picture garden plan. A purposeful planting. The work of His hands. As individuals, we are precious to God . . . but we are also a part of the whole. He did not plant us in isolation. And we are not the center of His world. The end goal of our planting is not simply for our own enjoyment and prosperity. Our place in history and location in geography are no accident. You and I have been personally planted and perfectly placed exactly where we are for a reason: to display the glory of God to those around us.

We see this truth way back in Genesis through the command to be fruitful and multiply (Genesis 1:28). He gives it again in His covenant with Noah (Genesis 9:1) and with Israel (Genesis 35:10). To Abraham, God promised to make him extremely fruitful (Genesis 17:6). And the heart of the Ten Commandments and the rest of the Law given to Moses for God's people, is for the thriving of both the individual and the nation. And while this charge to be fruitful and multiply certainly includes the bearing and raising up of children who know and love God, this command is not primarily one of physical fruitfulness. It is a spiritual fruitfulness. The heart of the commands of both the Old and New Testament is that of our spiritual growth. God has given us the recipe for living a spiritually fruitful life, in order that we would be fruitful followers of God. His plan has always been for our flourishing and so that He may be glorified. This is why we exist, to give God glory with the way we live our lives, because it is through the beautiful blooming of the Happy Soul that others see her heavenly Father.

> The Spirit of the Lord God is on me,
> because the Lord has anointed me
> to bring good news to the poor.
> He has sent me to heal the brokenhearted,
> to proclaim liberty to the captives
> and freedom to the prisoners;
> to proclaim the year of the Lord's favor,
> and the day of our God's vengeance;
> to comfort all who mourn,
> to provide for those who mourn in Zion;
> to give them a crown of beauty instead of ashes,
> festive oil instead of mourning,
> and splendid clothes instead of despair.
> And they will be called righteous trees,
> planted by the Lord
> to glorify him.
>
> Isaiah 61:1–3

The Old Testament is filled with prophecy, the foretelling of truths to come. These verses foretold much about Christ, the promised Messiah who would come to earth to rescue His people.

Jesus will bring good news to the poor.

Jesus will bring healing to the brokenhearted.

Jesus will bring liberty to the captives.

Jesus will bring justice, comfort, beauty, rejoicing, and hope.

We are the poor, the brokenhearted, captives in need of great help. This is the point where many teachers and preachers, books and blog posts might tell you that Jesus loved you so much that He gave up everything to come to earth and rescue you. And He did. But this is not the end of the story. There is more. And while Jesus indeed loves us with a great love, and this love was one big factor for why He came to earth, it is not His primary motivation; it is not His ultimate purpose. What Isaiah foretold as the purpose of why Jesus came (and the purpose Jesus himself stated again and again for coming) was for the glory of the Lord our God.

Do you see it there, tucked away at the end of this Isaiah passage? It's the very last part: "to glorify him." The good news is proclaimed to us—the bound and the mourning, the faint and the brokenhearted—so that we might be a "righteous tree, planted by the Lord," so that we can "glorify him." God has rescued us from our hopeless state, gifted us new life, and firmly planted us. All this for His glory.

The end goal of Jesus' coming was not our rescue.

The end goal of our salvation is not our salvation.

The end goal of becoming a Happy Soul is not simply being a Happy Soul.

The end goal of Jesus' coming was God's glory.

The end goal of our salvation is God's glory.

The end goal of becoming a Happy Soul is God's glory.

The Happy Soul exists to bring God glory.

This is the piece we often miss. Yes, we are recipients of mercy. Yes, we are beneficiaries of grace. But the implications of these truths are not to simply give us a healthy self-esteem. What is true of us because of Christ is not the end of the story. All of what God has done for us is for a greater purpose than just our salvation. The rescue of our souls from sin and the bestowing of every spiritual gift were all done for His glory. We have been saved to be a reflection of our Savior. The Happy Soul gets this, and it shapes everything she does—and doesn't do—because the Happy Soul exists to bring God glory.

I am a recipient of deep mercy.
I am a beneficiary of glorious grace.
I exist to bring glory to God.

> Let everything that breathes praise the Lord.
> Hallelujah!
>
> Psalm 150:6

13

Pursue Your Purpose

Pay careful attention, then, to how you live—not as unwise people
but as wise—making the most of the time, because the days are
evil. So don't be foolish, but understand what the Lord's will is.

Ephesians 5:15–17

Before Chris and I started dating, we were really good friends.
We enjoyed each other's company and could chat easily about all
sorts of things. Plus, we were both night owls. I worked second
shift at the hospital and often got home around 11:30 p.m. He and
I lived in the same apartment complex, and the apartment I lived
in was sort of the hangout hub, so I would typically come home to
a full house. One by one, my four roommates would head to bed,
and our other guests would head home, leaving Chris and me still
up chatting about the day. We had a comfortable, uncomplicated
friendship, facilitated by the fact that we both had our hearts set on
other people. I loved that I didn't have to worry about what signal

I was giving him, or what Chris might be trying to communicate to me. I knew he liked someone else, and he knew the same about me.

Until one morning, I woke up and realized I liked Chris Orr. I was so mad. Seriously. It felt like the end of a beautiful era. From that moment on, I struggled with knowing what to do and say. Over the next few months, I was consumed with navigating my newfound feelings but committed to waiting on the Lord. I didn't want to make the same mistakes I had in the past. I felt unable to trust myself. Then one day, it seemed as if something had changed. The space between us seemed to become more intimate and personal. But I refused to manipulate, "make a move," or force something to happen that wasn't supposed to happen. One night we finally had our "DTR"—define the relationship—talk. Chris initiated it, stating his feelings for me, and I spilled the beans on my own. We decided to take a week to pray about it and seek counsel from others.

The week went by, and Chris asked me out on an official date, which was really weird since we were already so comfortable with one another. He had planned a sweet and special evening. I was expecting something like dinner and a movie, so when he brought me down to the moonlit St. Johns River, stated his intentions to pursue me in a dating relationship with the view toward marrying me, it definitely astonished me. He had even typed out the characteristics of the Proverbs 31 woman and rewritten it to show how he saw each of those traits in me. Then he prayed for me and us and our potential future together. It was an incredibly romantic and thoughtful evening.

Going into that first date, I knew that I loved Chris. I knew that he was a man of godly character and biblical conviction. We were heading in the same direction, and I was 90 percent sure this was probably going to end in marriage. Furthermore, there were no physical ties to muddy the waters, as we had done nothing more than hold hands. He had just blown me away with this very special and intentional beginning to our dating relationship. Yet as we walked hand-in-hand back to his car, I was absolutely *freaking out.* I was so afraid that I had just made the biggest mistake of my life. What if this was not "the one" God had planned for me? What if this was not God's will for my life? I was paralyzed by the thought that I'd somehow misheard God and was going to mess my life up. It left me sick for days.

You're probably wanting to throw this book at me for being so stupid. From the outside looking in, our dating story sounds like a dream come true. I was so hyper-focused on God's particular will for my life, that I took my eyes off God's faithfulness and sovereignty. Did I no longer believe that God was in control? Did I not think God could stop me if I had indeed made a mistake?

This was not the first or last time I would become hyper-focused on God's very specific will for my life as I approached other decisions, especially when it came to motherhood:

Epidural or water birth?

Cloth diapers or disposable?

Public school or homeschool?

Stay at home or work full time?

During many of those seasons of searching, I spent tons of time researching and planning to figure out which decision to make, all while I neglected the reading of God's Word and the sitting at His feet. I was consumed with the pursuit of the ideals, and it led me to depression. I sought the "right" answer from God more than I sought God himself. I had to have the correct decision more than I cared about righteous living. I pursued the details within my role as a mother and neglected many of the details of my role as a child of God. Perhaps you've been consumed with decisions like these in your own life. Maybe they include one of the following:

Where should I go to school?

Which career path should I pursue?

Should I buy a house or rent one?

When should I retire?

All of these (and more) boil down to the same question: What is God's will for my life? This is not a bad question to ask. It is right to seek out God's will for the large and small areas of our lives. Yet so often we *obsess* over the specific answer to these questions and skip right over that which is black and white in Scripture. We ignore the following of God's clear plan for every Christian in order to hyper-focus on that which is specific only to our situation. When we do this, we miss the point of following God's will altogether.

I have found that the more I focus on God's clear and universal calling, the less I worry about the specifics. God's clear and universal calling is that which is clearly spelled out in Scripture and fits for every person, in every season of life, in every geographical region, and every time in history. It is crucial that we first clarify the difference between our "Big C" Callings and our "little c" callings. Both are important, but they must be pursued in order.

Our "Big C" Callings: The Universal Call on All of God's People

> So don't be foolish, but understand what the Lord's will is.
>
> Ephesians 5:17

The Bible is not a collection of random stories and commands. It is a masterpiece filled with movements of themes. The more you study it, the more you begin to see these themes. Though the Bible was written and compiled through the voices of many, it is all spoken from one voice. God's Word to us is united. God's call on our souls is as well. Here are four main points I see in Scripture to which God has called every Christian to spend their lives fulfilling. I've gathered them into a CALL acronym for us.

C—Conform: Know who God is and become more like Him.

A—Abide: Be intentional to remain in God's presence, God's precepts, and with God's people.

L—Labor: Work to use every gift of grace.

L—Launch: Be active in bringing the glory of God to our neighbor and the nations.

We've talked about much of this already. Together, they sum up the lifework of every past, present, and future Happy Soul. Let's take a look at each of our "Big C" Callings.

> Teach me to do your will,
> for you are my God.
> May your gracious Spirit
> lead me on level ground.
>
> Psalm 143:10

Conform: Know who God is and become more like Him

Put on your new nature, and be renewed as you learn to know your Creator and become like him.

> Colossians 3:10 NLT

But as the one who called you is holy, you also are to be holy in all your conduct; for it is written, Be holy, because I am holy.

> 1 Peter 1:15–16

We've already established that how we view God is the most important thing about us. It is critical because it affects the way we respond to Him. Another important reason why we need to pursue a right view of God is because over and over again in the Bible we are encouraged to be like Him. We cannot be like Him if we don't accurately know Him.

The more we rightly understand who God is and all He has done for us, the clearer our purpose in life becomes. We have been rescued to be a reflection of His character. And though we've been rescued from the sin-poisoned soil we used to live in, sin is still a threat to our flourishing. We must be vigilant—deliberate and determined to protect our soil.

Because our holy God has saved us, we get to be holy image-bearers to those around us. We must "lay aside every hindrance and the sin that so easily ensnares us" (Hebrews 12:1). As recipients of mercy and beneficiaries of grace, we have been given a new identity as an adopted child of God. The imprint of God is part of our very soul. Our attitudes and actions ought to be tied to God's attributes.

Be merciful, just as your Father also is merciful.

Luke 6:36

Just as the Lord has forgiven you, so you are also to forgive.

Colossians 3:13

Be perfect, therefore, as your heavenly Father is perfect.

Matthew 5:48

Therefore, be imitators of God, as dearly loved children, and walk in love, as Christ also loved us and gave himself for us, a sacrificial and fragrant offering to God.

Ephesians 5:1–2

So yes, the Bible is clear: The Happy Soul is called to know God and conform to His image.

> And just as we have borne the image of the man of dust, we will also bear the image of the man of heaven.
>
> 1 Corinthians 15:49

Abide: *Be intentional to remain in God's presence, God's precepts, and with God's people*

Our hearts are not good at abiding. Instead, they are prone to wandering. We need the constant attachment to God's presence, the changeless guiding of God's Word, and the continual encouragement of God's people to stay where we ought to be. We've already spent much time on the importance of God's presence and the role of God's Word in our lives. Yet this third piece—remaining with the people of God—is often neglected. These three—God's Spirit, God's Word, and God's church—are inexplicably linked. We cannot fully know, love, and worship God without the instruction of the Word of God and the community of His people. We cannot rightly understand and apply the Bible without the illuminating presence of God and the encouragement of the church.

Being a member of a local church is often thought of as an optional excursion instead of an integral part of the journey. Rather than being the default for those who know and love God, commitment to the local church has become a seasonal pursuit. *When travel baseball season is over, all the laundry is completed, and I'm all caught up on sleep, I'll go to church. As long as being a part of the church doesn't cramp my style, step on my toes, or ask too much of my time and energy, I'll be there.*

Why is it that we are more concerned about keeping up with our hair and nail appointments, accelerating our kids' sports stardom, and keeping our laundry baskets empty than we are in fulfilling the call to a body of believers? Now, I know that you may have had a bad experience in church. You may have been deeply wounded by people in the church. I have as well. As a pastor's wife, I'm often privy to the ugliness of people most churchgoers never see. Some of the largest, most hurt-filled wounds I've received have been from church members and their actions toward me or my husband. I get it. Some people are rude and petty. Some leaders have bad motives and big egos. But here's the lesson I've had to learn: Other people's sin doesn't give me the license to be disobedient. I am still called to be an integral part of a local congregation of believers. Let's not let the sinful mistakes of others be the excuse for our own.

So often we totally miss the point of why we're gathered together in the first place. The church doesn't exist to entertain. The church exists to proclaim the name of Christ. And that call to reflect the mercy and grace of God to those around us includes to each other. Think about this: So many commands in the Bible are communal commands. They are ones that assume you are around and committed to other believers. The context for the entire Bible is that of community—face-to-face, known-by-name, authentic, sacrificial community.

Biblically speaking, there is no such thing as a flying-solo Christian.

> Carry one another's burdens; in this way you will fulfill the law of Christ.
>
> Galatians 6:2

> But encourage each other daily, while it is still called today, so that none of you is hardened by sin's deception.
>
> Hebrews 3:13

> And let us watch out for one another to provoke love and good works, not neglecting to gather together, as some are in the habit

of doing, but encouraging each other, and all the more as you see the day approaching.

Hebrews 10:24–25

Therefore, as we have opportunity, let us work for the good of all, especially for those who belong to the household of faith.

Galatians 6:10

The New Testament is filled with teaching on God's church. Beyond all that we can learn from the snapshots we have of the early church in Acts, Scripture also teaches us the characteristics, expectations, and responsibilities of the church. There are four main pictures painted for us to help us understand the role the Happy Soul plays in the life of the church and the role the church plays in the life of a Happy Soul.

The church is the body of Christ

Now as we have many parts in one body, and all the parts do not have the same function, in the same way we who are many are one body in Christ and individually members of one another.

Romans 12:4–5 (See also 1 Corinthians 10:16–17, 12:12–14, 27; Ephesians 4:1–6, 11–16, 5:23, 30; Colossians 1:24.)

The church is the bride of Christ

Husbands, love your wives, just as Christ loved the church and gave himself for her.

Ephesians 5:25 (See also 2 Corinthians 11:2–3; Ephesians 5:25–29; Revelation 19:7–8, 21:9.)

The church is the family of God

Therefore, as we have opportunity, let us work for the good of all, especially for those who belong to the household of faith.

Galatians 6:10 (See also Matthew 12:49–50; John 11:52; 2 Corinthians 6:18; Ephesians 2:19; 1 Timothy 5:1.)

215

The church is the house of God

I have written so that you will know how people ought to conduct themselves in God's household, which is the church of the living God, the pillar and foundation of the truth.

> 1 Timothy 3:15 (See also Ephesians 2:19–22;
> 1 Corinthians 3:16; Hebrews 3:4–6; 1 Peter 2:5–7.)

We cannot live the Happy Soul life without a commitment to the body of Christ. We were not created to live our Christian life in isolation. We need each other. Just as no part of our own physical bodies can be cut off and survive on its own, so no part of the spiritual body of Christ can survive on its own. God has given us the church—the bride of Christ—for mutual encouragement, protection, and building up. If you allow any and every excuse to keep you from going to church, you are missing out on a major benefit of being a child of God. You will pass right over spiritual growth that will only come about as a result of being an integral part of the local church. Without it, you will be underdeveloped and overexposed to disaster.

The Happy Soul is called to abide—to dwell in God's presence, follow God's precepts, and be with God's people.

Labor: *Work to use every gift of grace*

For this very reason, make every effort to supplement your faith with goodness, goodness with knowledge, knowledge with self-control, self-control with endurance, endurance with godliness, godliness with brotherly affection, and brotherly affection with love.

> 2 Peter 1:5–7

When Chris and I prepared for our wedding we set up a gift registry. We got loads of everyday items we still utilize today:

silverware, plates and bowls, toaster, mixer, and more. But we received much (some we registered for while others were interesting, unsolicited gifts) that we don't use at all. For example, there is a set of crystal wine glasses that have never been used in our sixteen years of marriage. They sit high upon a shelf in their original box.

When we first came to Christ, we were given many gifts of grace: the Holy Spirit within us (Ephesians 1:13), the armor of God (Ephesians 6:10–18), every spiritual blessing (Ephesians 1:3), and so much more. Yet many of those gifts lay high on a shelf, never to be used. In his second letter to the church, Peter tells us that God "has given us very great and precious promises, so that through them [we] may share in the divine nature" (2 Peter 1:4). We have everything we need to live a godly life. Peter then tells us to "make every effort" to use all we have through Christ, "for if you possess these qualities in increasing measure, they will keep you from being useless or unfruitful in the knowledge of our Lord Jesus Christ." We are to work hard at utilizing all the gifts we have through Christ. Paul echoes this idea when he teaches us to "work out your own salvation with fear and trembling" (Philippians 2:12) and through "bringing holiness to completion in the fear of God" (2 Corinthians 7:1).

The Bible is filled with commands, and those commands are filled with actions. Put on. Lay aside. Set your minds. Draw near. Hold fast. Devote yourself. Be patient. Be persistent. Stand firm. Give thanks. Act wisely. Pay attention. Admonish. Comfort. Help. Submit. Love. Give. Rejoice. Pray.

We have work to do. The Happy Soul is actively engaged in working out her salvation. To do so, she utilizes the gifts of grace she's received from her Savior.

Launch: *Be active in bringing the gospel to the nations*

In the same way, let your light shine before others, so that they may see your good works and give glory to your Father in heaven.

Matthew 5:16

Here we come back to the purpose of our planting. The reason we exist. Many call this the "Great Commission"—the evangelistic task Jesus charged us to complete (Matthew 28:18–20). We have been given a high and holy calling to live our lives for the glory of God. We are called to live life with the big picture always in mind. This calling is intrinsic throughout the Word of God, but we often skip right over it without noticing. The Happy Soul lives a *therefore, since, because, so that* life. Everything we do is in response to God's rescue and for God's glory.

We are "a chosen race, a royal priesthood, a holy nation, a people for his possession, *so that* you may proclaim the praises of the one who called you out of darkness into his marvelous light." We are to live in holiness as pilgrims on our way to our new home in heaven, *so that* others "will observe your good works and will glorify God" (1 Peter 2:9, 12, italics added).

Go into all the world and preach the gospel to all creation.

Mark 16:15

Our "little c" callings: The Specific Call Given by God to Individuals

Beyond our "Big C" Callings, we each have an invitation into what I call our "little c" callings. Both types of callings are important. Both can be used for God's glory. But we need to make sure we keep them in order. Our "little c" callings are specific, seasonal, and subordinate.

Our "little c" callings are specific. They are specific to each of us and dependent on how God has built us and where He has placed us. This is where personality tests and knowing your spiritual gifts can be helpful. You are not like anyone on this earth. There are things only you can do the way you do them. As you figure out what God has made you good at, alongside of the experiences He's given you and the opportunities presented, there will be particular callings that present themselves throughout your lifetime that only you can fill.

Our "little c" callings are seasonal. These callings can come and go. You may be called to a particular line of work for a while but then be called to another later on. Perhaps you've been called to singlehood for a time. Maybe later God will bring you a spouse. Maybe not. Some women are called to marry. Some may become mothers, which opens up several different seasons of potential callings. Most married women eventually lose the love of their life. They then enter into a season of widowhood. Within each (and all those not mentioned), there are different ways of walking these paths, and God often calls us to a particular plan for a period of time and then on to another opportunity later.

Our "little c" callings are subordinate. Our secondary callings ought never to keep us from our primary callings. God will never call us into something that will bring us away from our primary callings. If our kids' activities keep us from being part of a local church, perhaps we need to reevaluate our priorities. If a relationship causes us to quit conforming to the holiness of God, perhaps the priority we're placing on that relationship needs some adjusting. If the lifestyle you *feel* called to keeps you from fulfilling any of your "Big C" Callings, this lifestyle is most likely not God's best plan for you. If your job consistently keeps you from opening God's Word and being with God's people, maybe there is a better job out there for you.

We must not live our lives with our callings upside down. Instead of ignoring them, let's be women who pursue our "Big C" Callings with all we have. Let's be sure that our "little c" callings are adding to—not taking away from—our "Big C" Callings. Our "Big C" Callings are not seasonal. We are not called to conform into the image of God seasonally. Our "Big C" Callings are not specific. The call to bring the gospel to the nations is not specific to only a few Christians. The *way* we are involved may look different, but we are all expected to be a part of fulfilling the Great Commission, starting in our own homes and neighborhoods, and at least through our giving and prayers for the nations. Our "little c" callings ought to complement our "Big C" Callings.

SOUL SEARCHING

Happy Soul Evaluation

How do I typically evaluate the callings of my life?
(Circle on the scale how you primarily view yourself.)

1........2.........3.........4........5..........6.........7..........8.........9.........10
I follow a self-proclaimed purpose   *I follow my God-given purpose*

How active am I in each of the following callings?

C—Conform: I know who God is and am becoming more like Him.

1........2.........3.........4........5..........6.........7..........8.........9.........10
Rarely think about this   *An active pursuit*

A—Abide: I am intentional to remain in God's presence, God's precepts, and with God's people.

1........2.........3.........4........5..........6.........7..........8.........9.........10
Rarely think about this   *An active pursuit*

L—Labor: I work to use every gift of grace.

1........2.........3.........4........5..........6.........7..........8.........9.........10
Rarely think about this   *An active pursuit*

L—Launch: I am active in bringing the glory of God to my neighbors and the nations.

1........2.........3.........4........5..........6.........7..........8.........9.........10
Rarely think about this   *An active pursuit*

Happy Soul Actions

Spend some time writing out all the roles you currently have (nurse, mom, caretaker, accountant, etc.).

_____

_____

_____

_____

_____

_____

Write out all your current commitments within and outside of these roles.

_____

_____

_____

_____

_____

Evaluate each of your roles and commitments by how they help or hinder the fulfillment of your "Big C" Callings. Consider reaching out to a friend or mentor who can help you chat through how you can make adjustments to pursue your "Big C" Callings more and more each day.

_____

_____

_____

_____

_____

_____

Happy Soul Prayer

Lord, help me see myself as you see me. Help me see my moments as you see them. Help me hold to an eternal perspective. Help me remember that this world is not my home. I need your vision, strength, and grace to walk toward a better fulfillment of all you've called me to do. Show me where I have been neglecting my "Big C" Callings. Give me a greater desire to use all I have and all I am for your glory, instead of my comfort and success. Help me see where my "little c" callings are for this season of life, and how these secondary callings can help me fulfill my primary callings. I want to be near you. I want my life to be used by you to bring your glory to those around me. Shape my mind. Change my heart. Make me into the specific Happy Soul you've created me to be.

SECRET #6

THE HAPPY SOUL
IS SURRENDERED
TO HER KING

14

Surrendered

How happy is anyone
who has put his trust in the LORD.

Psalm 40:4

For our fifteenth anniversary trip, Chris and I got to travel to Paris, France. It was a dreamy trip filled with breathtaking art, gripping history, stunning architecture, and incredible food. I can't wait to go back. While we were there, we saw all the must-see sights and visited all the typical venues (well, except for the Louvre . . . but that is a really sad story for another time). One of the highlights was climbing to the top of the Notre Dame cathedral towers. The view of the City of Lights was spectacular, and the up-close encounter with the stone gargoyles was exciting. The interior of the cathedral was full of its own brilliance. Though the majority of the thousands of people who slowly walked through the cathedral that day were not worshipers of Christ, there was a sense of awe on each observer. There was no running around or laughing. All words were spoken in a hush. The grandeur of the cathedral demanded a reverent silence.

Spectacular and awe-inspiring though it is, the cathedral of Notre Dame recently demonstrated its vulnerability when a fire took down some of the splendorous architecture. It was an unbelievable scene. The world watched in a different type of silence as centuries of history were consumed. Yet we ought not have been so shocked. The stories of yesteryear and the stunning edifice aside, what is the cathedral, really? It is simply a well-organized pile of wood and stone. Our hearts so quickly embrace the grandeur of the work of mankind, yet we gloss over the glory of the God who created the men who made that cathedral.

> All things were created through him, and apart from him not one thing was created that has been created.
>
> John 1:3

We've spent a lot of time looking at the main themes in Psalm 1, but there is much for us to see in Psalm 2 as well. The second psalm is a poem organized in four stanzas of three verses, each demonstrating a reality that points us toward the main thrust of the passage: God is King. So while it is appropriate for us to respond to the magnificence of the Cathedral of Notre Dame, it is important that we recognize that the grandeur of God our King demands our reverence too.

What Is Our Response to God's Rule?

> Why do the nations rage
> and the peoples plot in vain?
> The kings of the earth take their stand,
> and the rulers conspire together

against the Lord and his Anointed One:
"Let's tear off their chains
and throw their ropes off of us."

Psalm 2:1–3

You've probably heard of the "terrible twos," the season just about every toddler walks through. Filled with tantrums and tears, these two-year-olds are often found on the floors of the grocery store throwing a fit because they can't have the candy bars placed at their eye level. They are typically still learning how to communicate what they want and definitely still figuring out who's boss. Yet in the Orr household, the "terrible" two-year-olds have had nothing on our four-year-olds.

All three of my kids were absolutely defiant, incredibly assertive, and super self-centered at age four. They fought for independence at every step while simultaneously demanding more and more from Chris and me. If four-year-olds could have a Twitter account, their community hashtag when it comes to the authority figures in their lives would be #notmyboss. (Perhaps some teenagers hold to this hashtag as well?) They are marked by the refusal to submit to authority.

Tantrums aside, this type of declaration of defiance is common in the spiritual area of our lives. Instead of #notmyboss, we signal #notmygod every time we choose our ways instead of God's Way. I'm not talking about just those who refuse to trust Christ for salvation. We who claim the name of Christ declare #notmygod every time we choose our ways instead of His.

Psalm 2 begins with nations raging, peoples plotting, and a counsel of rulers declaring their rebellion to the law of the Lord. Submission is not an option, so they tune their hearts to the #notmygod channel and reject the "bonds" and "cords" of the way of the righteous. But just because they declare #notmygod doesn't make God any less God. The King of Kings has ruled, is ruling, and will rule forever in perfect righteousness. The Lord of all Lords is not threatened by their uprising, nor is His power hindered by their silly plans.

> The Lord frustrates the counsel of the nations;
> he thwarts the plans of the peoples.
> The counsel of the Lord stands forever,
> the plans of his heart from generation to generation.
> Happy is the nation whose God is the Lord—
> the people he has chosen to be his own possession!
>
> Psalm 33:10–12

One of my first small-group experiences was with several young women who met up once a week to study the Bible. I walked into that group thinking I knew a lot about God. I walked out of that group with an awareness that I was missing something. The other girls in the group talked about God like they'd just had coffee with Him earlier that day. They studied their Bibles daily. I opened up mine a few hours before our group started because I had forgotten to study it that week. They had a relationship with God. I had a reserve of information about God. They embraced God's Way. I treated God's Way as something to achieve. Yet I recently had been weary of God's Way. It was tiring and restrictive. It was beginning to seem pointless.

This awareness of my disparity compared to the other women in the group sent me searching for more. God, in His perfect timing, had placed me in a ministry that trained me how to study my Bible, and taught me all about Him and His plan for my life. For so long I had heard "Do, do, do!" and "Don't, don't, don't!" but very little about God himself. Before I entered that small group,

I had begun to despise all the do's and don'ts of God's Way and cast many of them aside for the pursuit of indulging my desire for sin. Gratefully, through the discipleship I received, I began to hear the why's behind the do's and the don'ts. Without the motivation—to know and be known by God—the good-girl list I had created held little sway on me once I let go of the pursuit of good. Without understanding that God's Way leads to God's presence, there was no incentive to follow the path proclaimed in the Bible. Before I gained the perspective of God as a personal, loving God who wants what is best for me, I called out with the Psalm 2:1–3 people, "Let's tear off [God's] chains and throw [His] ropes off of us!"

That time of my life set me on a course to seeing God the way those girls in my small group saw Him. As I began to see God for who He really is and understand how He views me—through the righteousness of Christ—I was gifted the ability to surrender. For the first time in my life, I saw God as both great and good, powerful and personal, awe-inspiring and near. Seeing and experiencing Him in a personal way led me to truly trusting Him with my life. I finally saw that surrendering to God leads to the greatest joy, the deepest peace, and the sweetest satisfaction my soul can hope for.

I thought that saying "yes" to surrender was agreeing to a restrictive list of do's and don'ts. Boy, was I wrong. Walking forward in surrender to God is the safest place I could ever be. Once I learned the secret to surrender and began following God simply to be with Him, my choices lined up with many of the guidelines I learned when I was young. The missing piece was intimacy with God. I thought that faith was a pursuit of perfection, when really, faith is a pursuit of a Person. Before surrender, my "faith" was full of actions with the goal of building my own shrine. After surrender, my faith is full of actions as an overflow of my heart's desire: to be nearer and nearer to the magnificent One who holds my life in His capable hands. Surrender is now a joyful running instead of a painful relenting. Surrender is a realization of who I am (beloved) and who I am not (a soul trying to prove its worth).

> Hallelujah!
> Happy is the person who fears the LORD,
> taking great delight in his commands.
>
> Psalm 112:1

God's Heavenly Throne Is Never Threatened

> The one enthroned in heaven laughs;
> the Lord ridicules them.[1]
> Then he speaks to them in his anger
> and terrifies them in his wrath:
> "I have installed my king
> on Zion, my holy mountain."
>
> Psalm 2:4–6

A reader-friend of mine suggested THE WHEEL OF TIME series to me several years ago. Containing fourteen books, this epic fantasy series is set in a medieval-like magical world full of courageous characters and engaging storylines. Each book follows the progressive unfolding of a prophecy and three main protagonists, one of which (I won't tell you which one because I hate spoilers, remember?) is proven to be the foretold Dragon Reborn. He is know as the Car'a'carn to one nation, and He Who Comes with the Dawn to others. He is also recognized as the Lord of the Morning, Prince of the Dawn, and True Defender of the Light. These titles—and the power, rights, and privileges bestowed on him through those titles—transformed a country child into a sovereign king of almost infinite power with one foretold blow. With the power of this new position behind him, the man known as the Dragon Reborn was able to unite many nations to serve him in a common goal to protect the world from certain doom.

Though our King—Everlasting God, Eternal Father, Prince of Peace, Lord of Lords, and King of Kings—holds many more titles, He is infinitely more powerful than any ruler we can imagine. His position is higher than any potential earthly authority. God, enthroned in heaven, is not threatened by any earthly attempts at attack. The declaration of the rebellious people in Psalm 2:3 who essentially stated, "We refuse to submit to your authority!" is met with God's own declaration: "I have been and will always be in control. My will cannot be thwarted." Unfortunately, more Christians liken the God of the Bible to a sweet Santa Claus than Majesty on High, King of Heaven, and Sovereign Lord. Yet Psalm 2 points our hearts to God's power and position, as does the rest of the book of Psalms (and the rest of Scripture).

His power is unlimited. His reach is unfathomable. His rule is unending.

This is the God deserving of our love. This is the God we were made to serve. This is the God we can wholeheartedly trust.

But for a very long time, this was not the god I had in my mind's eye. That god was weak, distant, and disinterested. So when prompted to surrender to Him, instead of running with abandon and joy into His warm and welcoming arms, I hid from the call and ran far away from what felt like unreasonable demands for more. I did not trust this god—the inaccurate one I had made up in my mind's eye. I couldn't imagine giving up control of my life to this weak and distant god. I really and truly thought that if I did surrender my all to this god, He would call me to let go of everything I held dear, because I thought that's what surrender was all about: I would have to say good-bye to everything I loved in order to say "yes" to this god.

I had it so very wrong. I had a loooong way to go in my view of God. But as my view of God grew, so did my view of surrender. I finally did learn the secret to surrender. In fact, I've done it a thousand times since. My life has taken turns I never dreamed it would. My life has been fuller and more fulfilling than I ever wished. Surrender is indeed a dying to self, a letting go of plans and dreams and control, but what I missed for so long is the fact that we do not surrender to be stripped down and left alone. When we submit to God, He doesn't take away everything we hold dear. Instead, He gives us that which can be held on to forever. Where I saw surrender as a scary proposition, in actuality it's been the safest proposal I've ever accepted.

> Blessed is the man who makes
> the LORD his trust,
> who does not turn to the proud,
> to those who go astray after a lie!
>
> Psalm 40:4 ESV

God's Power and Plan Cannot Be Hindered

> I will declare the LORD's decree.
> He said to me, "You are my Son;
> today I have become your Father.
> Ask of me,
> and I will make the nations your inheritance
> and the ends of the earth your possession.
> You will break them with an iron scepter;
> you will shatter them like pottery."
>
> Psalm 2:7–9

My oldest son has become interested in astronomy. The facts he uncovers and excitedly shares with me are absolutely mind-blowing. I have a hard enough time wrapping my brain around how many billions of people there are on this earth, so all the crazy-big numbers these super-smart scientists throw out are in another category altogether.

Though there is so much about this amazing planet we live on that points to the glory of God, if we zoom out to our solar system, the earth is minuscule compared to the size of Jupiter and Saturn. Zooming farther out, we see that our Solar System is just a tiny speck of the Milky Way galaxy (which astronomers estimate to contain somewhere between 200–400 billion stars). Yet our Milky Way is just one of many galaxies; there are estimated to be between 200 billion to 2 trillion other galaxies in the universe! Our God holds it all in place. Truly unfathomable.

> For everything was created by him,
> in heaven and on earth,
> the visible and the invisible,
> whether thrones or dominions
> or rulers or authorities—
> all things have been created through him and for him.
> He is before all things,
> and by him all things hold together.
>
> Colossians 1:16–17

> The heavens were made by the word of the Lord,
> and all the stars, by the breath of his mouth.
> He gathers the water of the sea into a heap;
> he puts the depths into storehouses.
> Let the whole earth fear the Lord;
> let all the inhabitants of the world stand in awe of him.

> For he spoke, and it came into being;
> he commanded, and it came into existence.
>
> Psalm 33:6–9

Yet our enthroned, powerful, magnificent, incomprehensible King also has personally given breath to every human that has existed and will exist on this planet. The hairs on every head have been numbered (Matthew 10:30). He sees every tear we have shed (Psalm 56:8). He discerns our thoughts, knows our every move, and is acquainted with our every way (Psalm 139:1–4). Not even a sweet sparrow falls to the ground without God's consent (Matthew 10:29). Nothing is impossible for the Lord (Genesis 18:14; Jeremiah 32:17, 27; Matthew 19:26; Luke 1:37). All current authorities have been allowed by God (Romans 13:1), and not one of His purposes can be stopped (Job 42:2).

In other words, He knows everything. He can do anything. And He is not threatened by anything mankind can throw His way. The headlines that scare us do not shake Him. Our King is in control—He is sovereign—and any puny little effort to rebel against Him is preposterous. Thus, God laughs at man's attempts to out-run His rule. The #notmygod campaign doesn't faze Him. In fact, though the nations plot an uprising, Psalm 2:6 tells us that "I have installed my king." It's in past tense. The deed is already done! His will cannot be thwarted.

> Oh, the depth of the riches and wisdom and knowledge
>   of God! How unsearchable are his judgments and how
>   inscrutable his ways!
> "For who has known the mind of the Lord,
>   or who has been his counselor?"
> "Or who has given a gift to him
>   that he might be repaid?"

> For from him and through him and to him are all things.
> To him be glory forever. Amen.
>
> Romans 11:33–36 ESV

What's Our Response to God's Invitation?

> So now, kings, be wise;
> receive instruction, you judges of the earth.
> Serve the LORD with reverential awe
> and rejoice with trembling.
> Pay homage to the Son or he will be angry
> and you will perish in your rebellion,
> for his anger may ignite at any moment.
> All who take refuge in him are happy.
>
> Psalm 2:10–12

Recognizing God as our King is such an important position to get settled in our hearts, because the command to "pay homage to the Son" is not simply to recognize mentally that He is in charge. The Bible tells us that even the demons believe in Him (James 2:19). Simple head-knowledge is not enough. The picture we see painted here is that of complete dedication, lifelong submission, and a moment-by-moment cherishing.

The word *submission* has the power to initiate in me a skedaddle sequence. I love control; the thought of giving it up is not naturally an attractive option. Deep down, surrender echoes images of failure—of giving up and giving in. A last resort. A desperate, arm-twisted-behind-my-back cry of relent, "Okay! Okay! Enough!" But surrender doesn't have to be a scary setback or a sign of failure. Relinquishing control can be a joy-filled sprint toward the greatest victory.

You and I have been chatting about a lot of potential change, and perhaps you're feeling a bit like I did: Change is impossible.

You might have noticed where you have some lopsided callings in your life and are seeing need for a rearranging of your priorities. Perhaps you're feeling utterly under the pile, giving in again to the lies that you will never be a "super-Christian" who fulfills all her "Big C" Callings. Maybe you are thinking the Happy Soul life is not what you are cut out for.

If you are feeling this way, know that you are in good company. Growing up, I heard the word *surrender* a lot. *Surrender your life to God* during chapel. *Surrender your life to God* at church. *Surrender your life to God* through the devotionals I read. They all pointed out my need to let go of my plans, trust in God, and follow God with everything I have. When I first began to entertain the idea of this life surrendered to God, I thought it would be the end of Katie. Surrender would be an inconvenient interruption—a detour from my plans.

My life's aspiration was to be the best. The best looking. The best friend. The best student. (You get the picture.) Deep down, I think I knew those pursuits were fleeting and futile. No one can be the best at everything and, even if it were possible, it couldn't be forever. There would always be someone closing in to one-up me. However, the challenge and the satisfaction of the achievement was worth the fight. So when this whole surrendering-my-life-to-God notion began to pull at my heart, it frightened me. Surrender would mean giving up the pursuit of being the best. And giving up being the best meant putting my identity on the line. If I wasn't the best, who would I be?

I didn't get that I already had an identity, and it is much better, much more fulfilling than chasing down the ideal. I still struggle with this. I forget that I am already a Happy Soul. I don't need to prove myself. I don't need the acceptance and recognition of others. I don't need to go out and make a name for myself. I've already been named.

אַשְׁרֵי!

Happy!

This is my identity. Already complete. Completely fulfilled. Fruitful. Resilient. Known. Righteous. This is your identity too. And as we choose to believe this to be true—regardless of how we feel and despite what our circumstances demand—our inward identity becomes our outward reality more and more and more. When we follow God in surrender and serve Him with all that we have, we make the choice to live as if God is indeed our King. As we recognize our need for the powerful, protecting presence of God in our every moment, and as we choose to hide ourself in Him as our home, we can confidently declare with the psalmist that "all who take refuge in him are happy."

15

Take Refuge

For the LORD God is a sun and shield.
The Lord grants favor and honor;
he does not withhold the good
from those who live with integrity.
Happy is the person who trusts in you,
LORD of Armies!

Psalm 84:11–12

Last summer my sister and her family came down to visit. It was their first trip to see us since we moved back to Florida. Some of her kids had never been to the beach and were excited to see the ocean and play in the waves and sand. So we packed up both minivans with chairs, a pop-up tent, a cooler full of food and drinks, and all the other assorted beach items you'd expect. Central Florida summers are known for their midafternoon storms, which typically bring a quick downpour and leave behind a sauna-level humidity. We'd been checking the weather reports all week leading up to our beach day. The forecast showed a light rain coming in the early evening, but nothing major and probably something that would come after we'd planned to leave.

About 2:00 p.m. the sky south of us started turning dark. We checked the app, and a small cell showed up but looked to be heading away from us and would likely bypass us. There were several other groups on the beach who had started packing up, like we had, as soon as the storm seemed imminent, but no one expected what was about to happen. Those dark skies that looked to be forever away were suddenly upon us. With them came a torrential downpour of cold rain and horrifying lightning, whose thunder we heard with a zero-seconds delay. We were officially caught in the middle of a strong summer storm—four adults in flip-flops with nine kids and enough stuff to fill the back of a truck. We attempted to dash back to the parking lot, but it was half a mile down the boardwalk, which skirted the nature preserve, and before we could get very far, the storm strengthened. Then it seemed to slow down and just sit on top of us.

There were two very small gazebos along the boardwalk. My brother-in-law Barry and four of the kids made it to the second shelter, which was only about a quarter of the way back to our minivans. My sister, mom, me, and the remaining cousins were stuck on the beach under the wooden stairs, where water and sand dripped down on our heads. One by one we made it up to the first portico, which kept the windswept sand out of our eyes, but the rain was coming in sideways and the lightning was way too close for comfort. It felt like we were stuck there for hours. Our only hope was to wait it out and pray the small shelter we found ourselves under would protect us from lightning. The adults were terrified, the kids were freaking out, and there *may* have been one who ended up with soiled britches.

Needless to say, my nieces and nephews no longer have a desire to go to the beach.

Standing in the middle of that storm, we all felt scared, vulnerable, and absolutely helpless. There was nothing we could do to change the nightmare we were living out. We had no safe space to land. No secure protection from the storm. We needed a refuge.

> My salvation and glory depend on God, my strong rock.
> My refuge is in God.
> Trust in him at all times, you people;
> pour out your hearts before him.
> God is our refuge.
>
> Psalm 62:7–8

To Take Refuge Is to Restfully Trust in Our King

In many ways, this is where it all comes together. All the Happy Soul secrets. All the Happy Soul actions. They begin and end here, with taking refuge in God. It starts with trusting in the charity of Christ for the salvation of our souls. It continues with trusting in the grace of God—in this "already but not yet" space—while we wait for our salvation to be complete. It starts with a correct view of God as our merciful rescuer. It continues with a correct view of God as our powerful sustainer.

> I am at rest in God alone;
> my salvation comes from him.
> He alone is my rock and my salvation,
> my stronghold; I will never be shaken.
>
> Psalm 62:1–2

The metaphor of taking refuge in God is central to the Psalms.[1] There are dozens of psalms that portray God as a refuge—a place where God's people can take cover from the storm and have no worry for their well-being. The original Old Testament audience would have clearly recognized this messaging through the usage of terms like *strong tower, rock, fortress, shelter, shield, stronghold,* and more. In a world without weather warnings and instant news updates, having a safe place nearby to run to in case of attack— whether that be from the enemy or from the clouds above—was a necessity for survival. Their world was continually filled with military and environmental threats; shelter from their potential foes was always sought out.

This refuge motif is also closely connected to the portrait throughout the Psalms of God as our King. In the book of Judges, there is a fable told that helps us understand the connection God's people would have had with taking refuge and kingship. In this Old Testament parable, a group sought a king, and one character who had been asked to reign over them replies to their requests: "If you really are anointing me as king over you, come and find refuge in my shade" (Judges 9:15). Taking refuge is the proof of trusting the kingship.

> The one who lives under the protection of the Most High
> dwells in the shadow of the Almighty.
> I will say concerning the LORD, who is my refuge and my
>   fortress,
> my God in whom I trust:
> He himself will rescue you from the bird trap,
> from the destructive plague.
> He will cover you with his feathers;
> you will take refuge under his wings.
> His faithfulness will be a protective shield.
>
> Psalm 91:1–4

As a college student, I served on Wednesday nights with a youth group the next town over. The church, established in 1837, had several buildings from several different eras, all of which were connected by hallways and unique spaces. One of these spots was my favorite for when we played hide-and-seek during youth lock-ins. It was a small space tucked under one of the stairwells. It was too small to store much in, but big enough that I could crawl into it, curl up, and relax while everyone else frantically found a good hiding spot. My spot was so good that one time I fell asleep and was woken up by the sound of several kids calling my name. They were trying to find me! The game had ended but I never showed back up to the youth room. That spot under the stairs was a safe space. It was my hide-and-seek refuge. I had surrendered to the safety of the spot, so much so that I had fallen asleep.

The Happy Soul is so convinced of the strength and faithfulness of her King that she readily takes refuge—seeks safety—under His protection. Once we have the goodness and grandeur of God settled in our minds, resting in Him comes much more naturally. It doesn't come perfectly, but it can become our preference. If we want the benefits of being in the shelter of God's wing, we have to let go of our plans and our "power" in order to rest. Being able to sit and rest under the shelter of God's safe plan and mighty hand recognizes that He is in control. He is able to see the big picture. He knows what has been and what will be. He loves me more than I can imagine. He has good plans for me.

> Then I called on the name of the LORD:
> "LORD, save me!"
> The LORD is gracious and righteous;
> our God is compassionate.
> The LORD guards the inexperienced;
> I was helpless, and he saved me.
> Return to your rest, my soul,
> for the LORD has been good to you.
> Psalm 116:4–7

To Take Refuge Is to Relinquish All to Our King

> Come to me, all of you who are weary and burdened, and I will give you rest. Take up my yoke and learn from me, because I am lowly and humble in heart, and you will find rest for your souls. For my yoke is easy and my burden is light.
>
> Matthew 11:28–30

I've already mentioned that I'm a city girl, but I love learning about farming—specifically how fields are planted and crops are gathered. Especially in "olden" times. When we lived in Kentucky, we took many field trips to Shaker Village, a restored community from the 1800s. In one of the old barns, they have antique farming tools on display, one of which is a large, wooden, handmade yoke meant to attach two animals together so they could work the land. Through the yoke, the weight of what they are pulling is distributed and the power of the partnership between those animals is harnessed.

Here in Matthew, Jesus is offering a great promise. If we yoke ourselves to Christ for the work ahead of us, it will be easier than trying it alone. He says His yoke is easy and light because He does all the heavy lifting. We simply need to stay close enough to stay in step with where He is leading us.

We have to stop trying to pull everything on our own. When we do, we say that we don't need God. When we fail to follow God's Way, we try to pull the cart of our life in our own power. When we neglect to delight in God's Word, we attempt to satisfy our souls with something that will leave us weary and war-torn. Jesus invites us to take up a yoke that is life-giving and not burdensome. But we have to lay down our self-imposed burdens to pick up His.

Surrender brings a realization that life is not about me. My life's purpose is not to follow my plans, my comfort, or my privileges.

The abundant life the Happy Soul is promised in Christ is experienced as she gives up the pursuit of self in order to serve her King. "If anyone wants to follow after me, let him deny himself, take up his cross, and follow me. For whoever wants to save his life will lose it, but whoever loses his life because of me will find it" (Matthew 16:24–25). Everything else—all the actions of the Happy Soul—follows this surrender of self. And this surrender starts with the death of self. But this death is a beautiful death. It's a freeing death. It's a victorious death. It's the realization that I can never achieve holiness on my own. I can never be a Happy Soul on my own.

The Happy Soul needs a King.

The Happy Soul serves that King with every breath she breathes.

The Happy Soul has abandoned autonomy.

The Happy Soul is resolved to renounce sin.

The Happy Soul has an unshakable union with Christ.

The Happy Soul has let go of entitlements to embrace an eternal perspective.

The Happy Soul holds a readiness to revere her King.

> But let all who take refuge in you rejoice;
> let them shout for joy forever.
> May you shelter them,
> and may those who love your name boast about you.
>
> Psalm 5:11

Now to the King eternal, immortal, invisible, the only God, be honor and glory forever and ever. Amen.

> 1 Timothy 1:17

SOUL SEARCHING

Soul Evaluation

How do I primarily view God's Way?

1....... 2....... 3....... 4....... 5....... 6....... 7....... 8....... 9....... 10
Restrictive chains   Love-filled boundaries

How confident am I that God's power and plan cannot be thwarted?

1....... 2....... 3....... 4....... 5....... 6....... 7....... 8....... 9....... 10
I'm a doubter   I trust Him completely

Where am I on the surrender spectrum?

1....... 2....... 3....... 4....... 5....... 6....... 7....... 8....... 9....... 10
Scared of it   Completely submitted

Happy Soul Actions

Spend some time journaling through the following questions:

Am I afraid of surrender? What is holding me back? In what areas of my life am I declaring #notmygod?

_____

_____

_____

_____

_____

_____

Share your hesitations to God through prayer.

_____

_____

_____

_____

_____

Go back through the chapters in this section and select a few passages you need to cling to about who God is. Write them out on 3x5 cards and keep them handy. Internalize them. Meditate on them.

_____

_____

_____

_____

_____

Write out a prayer to God and ask Him to allow your mind's eye to see a more accurate view of who He is.

_____

_____

_____

_____

_____

_____

Happy Soul Prayer

God, I am in awe of you. Please continue to give me a more accurate view of who you are. Show me your glory! Don't let me slip into an apathetic faith. Reveal to me the areas of my life where I am declaring #notmygod, where I neglect to follow your instructions and refuse to submit to your ways. I praise you for making a way for me to encounter you in intimate ways. I deserve your wrath. But I stand, in Christ, redeemed and justified. I praise you for this transformation.

The Happy Conclusion

Just this week I gave in to complaining in the worst way. I chose selfishness over sacrificing my petty desires for the sake of others. I dove into self-pity and anger. The fruit of God's Spirit within me has not been very evident. In other words, I don't have these secrets all perfectly worked out in my life. As long as my soul abides in this body, I never will.

I've learned not to freak out when I have a bad week. Yes, I need to repent and recognize my wrong. Yes, I can't stay here in the muck. But I've come to understand that starting over can begin any second. God is always awaiting my return, and He is always working—even when I am wasting time. And over time—lots of time—I can see growth. The kind of growth that you don't even know is happening until one day you take a fresh look and realize you've changed. Just like how I don't notice how my kids are growing because I see them all the time, but then I see a picture of them from just a few months back and I'm stunned at how much they've grown. Just like the tree in our Kentucky front yard that grew each year right under our noses. We saw it day after day and barely gave it a second glance, but when we compare pictures of the house from when we first moved in and when we finally moved out five years later, the change was dramatic.

The seasons of our spiritual growth often resemble the seasons our tree experienced through all the Kentucky weather changes. There are months of abundant growth, but there are also times where we wonder if we'll ever see the buds of spring again. Sometimes we experience bursts of fresh and exciting growth. Other times we go through a slow, strengthening season. Yet all along we are growing. Even if *today* is not a bursting-with-fruit sort of day, we can know that it *is* a day where we've been moved forward by God's working.

So don't give up. Don't give in to discouragement. Don't allow the feelings of failure or the paralysis of perfectionism keep you from moving forward. Believe better. Open your Bible. Enjoy it. Follow it. Abide in Christ. Remember who you are and where you are going. Fulfill your "Big C" Callings and engage in your "little c" callings. Rest in His safety and power. Remember. Remember. Remember.

One day, you will stand in Christ. Complete. A perfectly developed and beautifully fruitful tree. A completely Happy tree that displays the faithfulness and splendor of God.

You *will* be a complete and perfect Happy Soul.

Notes

Chapter One The Pursuit of Happiness

1. John Shryock, "'Very lethal dose' of poison likely to kill Toomer's trees," WSFA 12 News, February 16, 2011, https://www.wsfa.com/story/14043972/toomers-corner-trees/.

2. James A. Swanson, *A Dictionary of Biblical Languages with Semantic Domains: Greek* (Logos Bible Software, 2001).

3. Sears Archives, http://www.searsarchives.com/homes/index.htm.

Chapter Two Happy! The Name of God's People

1. Raegan Thornhill, "God Calls Us to Be Holy, Not Happy," *Whole Magazine*, October 25, 2017, www.wholemagazine.org/devotionals/god-calls-us-to-be-holy not happy, accessed Nov. 27, 2018.

2. Gary Thomas, *Sacred Marriage: What If God Designed Marriage to Make Us Holy More Than to Make Us Happy?* (Grand Rapids, MI: Zondervan, 2015).

3. John Piper, *Desiring God: Meditations of a Christian Hedonist* (Sisters, OR: Multnomah, 1996), 23.

4. R.C. Sproul, "The Key to the Christian's Joy," *Ligonier Ministries*, May 7, 2018, www.ligonier.org/blog/key-christians-joy/.

5. Albert Mohler, "The Osteen Predicament—Mere Happiness Cannot Bear the Weight of the Gospel," AlbertMohler.com, September 3, 2014, albertmohler.com/2014/09/03/the-osteen-predicament-mere-happiness-cannot-bear-the-weight-of-the-gospel/.

6. Joni Eareckson Tada, *More Precious Than Silver: 366 Daily Devotional Readings* (Grand Rapids, MI: Zondervan, 1998).

7. Joni Eareckson Tada, *More Precious Than Silver*, 263.

8. Online Etymology Dictionary, https://www.etymonline.com/word/awful.

9. Online Etymology Dictionary, https://www.etymonline.com/word/meat.

10. Online Etymology Dictionary, https://www.etymonline.com/word/bimbo.

11. Online Etymology Dictionary, https://www.etymonline.com/word/husband.

12. Online Etymology Dictionary, https://www.etymonline.com/word/sad.

13. Online Etymology Dictionary, https://www.etymonline.com/word/intercourse.

14. Swanson, *A Dictionary of Biblical Languages*.

15. George Eldon Ladd, *A Theology of the New Testament* (Grand Rapids, MI: Eerdmans, 1993), 368.

Chapter Three The Perfect Portrait of Happiness

1. Claus Westermann, *The Psalms: Structure, Content, and Message*, trans. Calver Verlag Stuttgart (Minneapolis, MN: Augsburg Publishing House, 1980), 10.

2. Tremper Longman, *How to Read the Psalms* (IVP, Logos version), 42.

3. Westermann, 12, 17.

4. Mark Futato, *Interpreting the Psalms: An Exegetical Handbook* (Grand Rapids, MI: Kregel Publications, 2007), 67.

Chapter Four Focused

1. C. S. Lewis, *Prince Caspian*, THE CHRONICLES OF NARNIA (New York: HarperCollins, 1994 edition), 141.

Chapter Eight Attached

1. C.S. Lewis, *Reflections on the Psalms* (San Francisco: HarperCollins, 2017), 68.

2. Andrew E. Hill and John H. Walton, *A Survey of the Old Testament* (Grand Rapids, MI: Zondervan, 2009), 175.

Chapter Nine Enjoy God's Word

1. I go into this idea in depth in my *Everyday Obedience* Bible study.

2. Colossians 3:9; Ephesians 4:22; Romans 8:13; Galatians 5:24, to name a few.

Chapter Fourteen Surrendered

1. This reference to the laughter and ridicule shown by God is an anthropomorphism. It is part of the imagery the poet sought to project. This is not meant for us to walk away thinking God sits in heaven laughing at and ridiculing people. Instead, it is meant to portray the futility of the people's attempts to divert God's plans.

Chapter Fifteen Take Refuge

1. Futato, *Interpreting the Psalms*, 97.

Join the

HAPPY SOUL SISTER COMMUNITY

For a virtual book club, Happy Soul stories,
and encouragement to walk out your Happy Soul identity,
join our private online community.

Secretsofthehappysoul.com/sisters
password: ash-ray

Katie Orr is passionate about helping women enjoy God daily. As a national conference speaker, prolific author, and online Bible coach, she provides biblical teaching and relevant resources to help women jump-start their journey toward walking with Jesus. A former Cru college minister, and mother to three, she and pastor-husband, Chris, serve together in the local church. Connect with Katie at katieorr.me and @thekatieorr on social media.

Share your own
Happy Soul journey with Katie
using the hashtag #happysoulbook.